Cancer

Cancer-
A Journey
through the
Valley

Rita Kroon

A Walk to the Well

Dedicated to:

*Each of you or your loved ones who have
heard the incomprehensible words
"You have cancer";
To my husband and my family who
give me reason to keep going on this journey;
To my friends and prayer warriors who stood
on the sidelines and cheered me on and
prayed without giving up; and
to Jesus because it is for His glory
that I write.*

Special Dedication

"In My Heart"

I thought of you today, Burt and René
but that is nothing new.
I thought about you yesterday
and the days before that too.
I think of you in silence;
I often whisper your names.
All I have now are memories
and your pictures in my frames.
Your memories are my keepsake
with which I will never part.
God has you in His keeping;
I have you in my heart.

Rita Kroon

Foreword

No matter what age a person may be when diagnosed with cancer, it can be a devastating time and truly a walk through the valley of the shadow of death. This is my story, but I hope you see it more than a story of one more person having cancer. My intent is that you will see God's faithfulness and His sovereignty as we journey through the trials of living on earth. We have hope! Romans 8:28 says: "And we know that God causes **all** things to work together for good to those who love God, to those who are called according to *His* purpose." (NAS) I hope you hear your own voice in my story as we travel together through the valleys to the mountain tops and everywhere in between. We need not fear, for His rod (protection) and His staff (guidance) comfort us.

Acknowledgements

Words could never express my love and devotion to my husband, Burt, for the tender care and support he has always shown me, especially during my season of cancer and every day since. He reflects the love and compassion of Jesus Christ, our Lord and Savior, in such a way that I am truly blessed.

With deep appreciation I would also like to thank my daughter, LaDawn, for her vital role with technology in the completion of this book. Through the ups and downs and the unglued times, she persevered. Thanks a bunch!

Table of Contents

Chapter 1

Things Aren't What They Seem

Weekends at our cabin on the Kettle River in central Minnesota brimmed with activity—grandkids and their friends four-wheeling through the woods, daughters and their husbands playing endless board games, and loud squeals from the adventurous swimmers answering the dare to jump into the cold water.

"I can't feel myself!" one grandson with blue lips hollered as he cannonballed into the river again.

But one particular July 4th weekend stood out from the rest. This time, my husband and I spent it alone at our cabin.

After a quiet and leisurely breakfast on the deck, I packed a picnic lunch in preparation for the day's celebration in Moose Lake sixteen miles away.

Thin tatters of clouds drifted across the immensely blue sky. Red-wing black birds twittered from the marsh nearby. It was a perfect summer day.

"Let's go down to the river before we head to town," I said.

Burt nodded with a smile.

We strolled down the path hand-in-hand in peace and solitude. The dark river glistened in the morning sunlight as though it carried millions of diamonds to unknown recipients downstream. The river splashed over rocks as though singing merrily on its way.

I leaned into Burt as he put his arm around my shoulders. "I love the sound of the river."

"This is nice," he said, quietly.

I looked up and smiled, but then I must have frowned.

"What's wrong?" he asked.

"I don't know." I rubbed my hand across my lower abdomen. "I feel crampy."

"When did that start?"

"Just now." My eyebrows pinched together. "And I think I have a fever."

We walked back to the cabin, and I took my temperature. "Barely a hundred," I said holding the thermometer out for him to see.

"Maybe we shouldn't go to the parade," he said.

"No, I'll be fine." I brushed aside the unusual ill feeling

Within a couple of hours, I felt back to normal.

Later, we sat on the curb at the beginning of the parade route as the gaily decorated floats and precision marching bands with drums and horns paraded before us. We scrambled for candy tossed in our direction and gave it to young children nearby scampering for their stash.

That evening, we headed to Finlayson for fireworks. I felt fine, and yet the thought of my crampy feeling earlier nagged at the back of my mind.

The following Tuesday, I thought about calling the doctor—more curious than concerned with my brief episode of feeling ill. I was in excellent health, and at age sixty I still walked three miles every day, ate healthy meals, didn't smoke, and didn't drink alcohol. *What could possibly be wrong? I should call to be on the safe side.*

The next day, I sat with my doctor in the exam room.

"I feel silly being here," I said. "I'm fine now. It was minor cramping and a low grade fever that lasted a few hours."

"Don't feel silly. It's perfectly reasonable to be concerned."

After examining me, he said, "I don't find anything out of the ordinary, but I would like you to have a CT scan of your abdomen."

Disturbing thoughts of danger began to simmer in the recesses of my mind. "Really?"

"Yes, only to make certain all is okay," Dr. Anderson said, with a reassuring smile.

When storm clouds gather on the horizon, I have learned the best place to take refuge is in prayer. I thought about the words I once heard, "Safety is not found in the absence of danger, but in the presence of God." Hmm. I know it is in the quiet realm of my heart where I am being shaped and molded for His purpose. "Keep me calm before you, O Lord."

On Thursday, Burt and I drove to a local hospital in downtown St. Paul for my CT scan.

The scan itself proved routine, but the phone call from the doctor was not.

"Something showed up on the CT in your left ovary area so I would like you to see an oncologist GYN," Dr. Anderson said. His voice sounded guarded. He gave me the name and number of the specialist I was to see.

I hadn't had any more episodes of cramping or fever, so I thought seeing an oncologist seemed a bit drastic. I trusted his judgment, however. I called and made an appointment for the following week. *So he's an oncologist. It's only a precaution. Why am I jumping to conclusions?*

I instinctively knew my path was mapped out before me, and yet, fear crept in and crowded out my fragile peace. "Please, Lord Jesus, help me to know You walk beside me."

Later, Burt and I sat quietly in the GYN surgeon's small consultation room, and waited. A middle-aged man with dark wavy hair walked in, introduced himself, and sat behind the desk. "Mrs. Kroon," he began slowly, "the CT shows a definite spot in your left ovary area."

He gave me a moment to absorb the preliminary results of the scan before continuing. "We need to talk about surgery."

So much for small talk. I nodded for him to go on as a feeling of apprehension nudged its way into my being.

"A complete hysterectomy is always a possibility," he explained, "but I won't know for certain until we do surgery."

My chest felt tight and my breathing became shallow. Burt's hand slid across my shoulders.

The doctor talked in length about the procedure and said his nurse would schedule surgery for July 26th—three weeks after my one and only episode of feeling a little ill. "Do you have any questions?" he asked.

 I shook my head.

After he left the room, I had a million questions, of course, but they stayed silent and unanswered in my mind.

In the weeks prior to surgery, I talked with friends who had hysterectomies and asked how they weathered their surgeries.

"Piece of cake!"

 "Best thing I ever did!"

"Wish I would've done it sooner!"

I began to feel a little more at ease.

But that confidence shattered in an instant when I called an out-of-town friend. She acknowledged that she heard my news, but then without taking a breath, she went on to tell me about a decorating project on which she had been working that had come together beautifully.

I emailed another friend about my upcoming surgery. *Somebody, please encourage me.* My friend replied, but she brushed past my circumstance. Instead, she wrote of the sale of their house and their plans to buy a new home.

The world continues to spin, but my world was beginning to crack.

What did Paul say? "For I have learned in whatever situation I am to be content...I can do all things through Him who strengthens me." (Philippians 4:11-13)

"Lord, give me strength."

Many times Burt and I prayed to be at peace and to trust in the Lord as we took our first steps into scary and unfamiliar territory.

"Dear Lord, please show me Your presence in such a way that I will know for certain that You are with me."

Several people across the nation, from California to Ohio to New York prayed on my behalf. I opened my Bible to Hebrews 2:13, "I will put my trust in Him."

Every journey begins with one step. "Lord, help me to trust you with my whole heart."

On the day of surgery, I was prepped and then waited in the pre-op area. My heart beat fast, and my palms felt sweaty as I tried to concentrate on what the anesthesiologist and the rest of the surgical team had to say before I headed into surgery.

After the five-hour surgery and an hour in recovery, I was brought to my room. Even though I lay in bed with a sore abdomen, I was glad to have the hysterectomy over with. My supper tray arrived moments before the surgeon did.

After usual pleasantries, the surgeon said, "I thought the left ovary was the culprit, but it was not your ovary at all. You did not have a hysterectomy."

"O my! What then?" I asked putting the metal lid back over my untouched food.

"You have a tumor that entangled itself in the blood vessels, veins, artery, and nerves," the surgeon explained in a gentle tone.

I tried to swallow, but I had no saliva. A tumor? I felt like I was in the throes of a dense fog. I tried to concentrate on what the man in blue scrubs was saying.

Burt moved from his chair to the edge of my hospital bed.

"I took what I could, but I left a margin," he finished apologetically.

A margin?   What does that mean?   I stared at him waiting for this absurd report to sink in.

"What now?" Burt's voice sounded strained.

"We'll do a biopsy of the tumor and we'll know more by Mrs. Kroon's follow-up visit in two weeks. In the meantime," he said turning to me, "rest and try to get your strength back."

At my follow-up appointment, no sooner had Burt and I sat down in the consultation room when the surgeon stepped in. He looked somber.

"Keep me calm before You, Lord.   Help me to breathe."

The doctor's voice was low. "Mrs. Kroon, you have cancer." He paused. "It's a rare cancer called leiomyosarcoma located in the retroperitoneal area."

I was numb to the reality of what he was saying. He might as well have been speaking Greek. Disbelief coupled with anxiety swept over me like a suffocating tidal wave. While my mind swirled to grasp the magnitude of his words, I heard his voice continue. "…I recommend you have twenty five radiation treatments over a five week period."

Our marriage vows spoken thirty-nine years earlier, "To have and to hold in sickness and in health until death parts us" never specified the enormity of adjustment there would be when dealing with cancer. But now we had to adjust. No longer could we carelessly consider good health as a thing to be taken for granted.

I mumbled something to the effect that I would let him know. I couldn't think. Not now. I could not bear to remain in that room one more minute! I wanted to run and never stop. I wanted to get as far away as possible from those words, "You have cancer!"

Once out in the car, Burt and I sat in silence. Not an awkward silence, but a silence that's shared deep within. We groped for words, but we could not speak. We both reeled at the magnitude of the doctor's words. Tears flowed freely for both of us.

After several minutes of each of us locked in our emotions trying to grasp the unimaginable, Burt drew me close to him and held me as we sobbed together.

"Cancer." I said the word, but my mind could not wrap itself around the implications of that dreadful and alarming word. And radiation? It didn't seem like the right direction for me. Nothing seemed right.

"Dear Father in heaven, this is too much to process. Please help me," were the only words I could utter.

If there were people and traffic and trees outside our car, I was not aware of them. All I knew in that moment was that I took the Lord's hand and stepped onto the battlefield.

Chapter 2

Amazing Email

After a few days, the reality of the doctor's diagnosis of cancer began to settle in, but turmoil over five weeks of radiation rose up. I felt extremely restless and seemingly unable to move forward with the doctor's recommended treatment. *Where do I start? What do I do? What are the side effects?* It was as though I stood at the edge of a deep, raging river and must cross to the other side. *Do I swim? Walk the bridge? Ride the ferry? How do I get there?*

I spent the day in intermittent prayer and racing thoughts. Burt and I prayed together, and I spent an unknown amount of time alone in prayer. "O Lord God, Maker of heaven and earth, the heavens are full of Your glory and the earth displays Your handiwork. You have redeemed me and made me Your child. Please, Father, show me what You would have me do. I am in strange territory, and I do not know the way. Your Word says that You are a very present help in time of need and if ever I needed You, it is now."

I wanted to know what I was dealing with so I looked up leiomyosarcoma on line. I gathered all the information possible to better equip myself so I could understand more fully what I was facing.

I learned that my cancer, leiomyosarcoma (LMS), is a rare, cancerous, soft- tissue tumor that originates from smooth muscle cells. I read that only four people in a million have this type of cancer. Therefore, not much research and data had been collected. I stared at the computer monitor when I read that LMS usually does not respond to chemo and only minimally to radiation. No matter how many times I re-read this medical blurb, I could not begin to grasp its significance.

I did not want to be labeled by a rare cancer. I thought I believed that Jesus was my everything, but then, I wondered. *Is it Jesus and my health? Jesus and my family? Jesus and my whatever word filled the blank? When one or more of these is taken away, was Jesus indeed my all-in-all?* Difficult thoughts I had to honestly consider.

I cupped my chin in my hand and my shoulders slumped as I noted with much chagrin that LMS is an angry cancer, and that it usually claims its victim sooner or later with only a two per cent survival rate. Although there were a few success stories along the way, all in all, it was not an encouraging prognosis. I checked my options and other than surgery, I did not seem to have any. *Well, I've already had surgery*, I thought, *so now what? More surgery?*

Again, I wanted to be informed as much as I possibly could be, so I looked up radiation. I discovered that if I had radiation, and my cancer came back in the same area, I could not repeat radiation treatment. I felt like I was walking down a long, narrow hallway with no doorways. *I don't want to be here.*

Throughout the entire next day, unsettled and unsure, I paced from room to room in our modest home. I prayed earnestly and constantly for the Lord's direction. I was perplexed as to why it seemed like I was up against an invisible wall that prevented me from going forward with radiation.

That night, I listened to Burt breathe softly, but sleep eluded me as I wrestled in my quandary. I know our heavenly Father loves His children much too much to leave us unattended, and so I waited. The words of 1 Thessalonians 5:17 came to mind. "Pray without ceasing. Give thanks in all circumstances for this is the will of God in Christ Jesus for you." I prayed constantly. I tried to give thanks for the many blessings.

Early Thursday morning, Rob, my brother two years my senior, called. "Go check your email," he said.

"Why?"

"Just check your email," he urged.

He had told me the day before that he had a co-worker who had a sister in Florida that also had leiomyoscaroma. Four in a million and now I knew two of us. I told Rob that I would check my email and get back to him.

I still felt apprehensive as I opened my email and there it was—an email from a total stranger in Florida. She wrote, "If you have any doubts about a doctor's treatment plan, listen to your heart. Get a second opinion." She went on to write, "There's a world-renowned place called Mayo Clinic in Rochester, Minnesota. It looks like it's about 85 miles from St. Paul. Call them. I wish you well. Geri"

The instant I read her words, I felt a calm settle over me like someone had draped a shawl around my shoulders. I had my direction! "Thank You, Lord, for showing me the way," I whispered as hope began to surge within me.

I re-read her message and thought; *bless her heart. Here is someone in Florida with LMS telling me about Mayo Clinic here in Minnesota. How incredible!*

I called Mayo Clinic, and to my amazement, I secured an appointment the following week. They would send me an itinerary of appointments for blood work and a full CT scan, and a meeting with an oncologist. But in the meantime, "Could you gather all your records and films and slides from your surgery and bring them with?" said the female voice on the other end.

15

I called Rob back and thanked him for handing the baton to his co-worker who handed it to his sister in Florida who handed it to me. I now had the baton and would run with it. I had a mission!

I drove to the area hospital where I had surgery and hurried from department to department with my request to round up my records. I stopped at the pathology department to pick up the actual slides of the biopsy of my tumor. At my request, the lady on the other side of the window disappeared behind a wall of file drawers. When she returned, she looked puzzled.

"They are not here."

"Oh my," I gasped. "But I need them for an appointment next week at Mayo Clinic," I said in desperation.

"Let me see if I can track them down," she offered in an understanding tone.

Shortly thereafter, she said, "Huh. That's strange. Well, I did track down the whereabouts of the slides." She looked at me with raised eyebrows. "They are in Rochester at Mayo Clinic."

I stood in stunned silence. "Rochester?"

"Yes. They were sent there yesterday for further analysis."

I could hardly believe my ears. "Wow! This is incredible!" I said. "They are exactly where they should be."

She smiled, but she could not have possibly known the impact this had on me. "What a confirmation! Thank You, Lord Jesus. Thank You that You care about each detail of our lives," I whispered as I hurried back to my car.

That same day, one of my dearest friends, Sharon, and her husband stopped by to visit. "Will you have time to read this?" she asked, as she handed me a book— *It's Not About Me* by Max Lucado. She explained that according to Lucado, "God does not exist to make a big deal out of us. We exist to make a big deal out of Him. It's not about you. It's not about me. It's all about Him," she quoted Lucado.

I hesitated, but then accepted the book. "I will read it," I said gratefully.

I pondered Lucado's words in his first chapter. *What do you mean, Lucado? It isn't all about me? Easy for you to say. I've been diagnosed with a rare cancer and I don't have any rabbits in my hat.*

But then, ever so slowly I began to realize the depth of this truth, and even though my appointment at Rochester loomed over the vista, my focus plodded ever so slowly from myself to God.

Beth Moore, author of several books and Bible studies, conveyed the same thought only in different words. "We make life so much more complicated when our approval of life is all about me because the rest of the world never cooperates! God is God, and frankly, it's all about Him. With God, it's all about us. We seek to please Him; He seeks to perfect us—and life works. Not without pain, but with purpose."

Life cannot be depicted by cancer or any other disease—no matter how deadly. Neither should life be characterized by pleasurable gifts such as family, sports, hobbies and talents, or iPods and Smart Phones. Life is defined by our relationship to Jesus Christ—a deep, personal, and authentic relationship.

I understood with certainty that no matter what circumstance in which we may find ourselves, God is sovereign. Even though I may not like where I am on God's map, I firmly believe that He knows, He cares, and He can be trusted. "As the moon reflects the greater light, soft light touches a dark earth," Lucado said.

The world is not about me. It's not about my cancer. What it is about is Jesus, Son of God, Son of man, and what He is going to accomplish in my life, in my faith, and in my emotions. Even though the world around me seemed to be spinning out of control, I began to grasp in a new and real way that God is faithful, and that God is sovereign.

I believe that God gives healing to those He desires. I also accept as true that He gives grace to sustain those for whom He has a different purpose. Either way, He has us in the palm of His hand. And that is comforting. If adversity draws us to Him, ought not comfort do the same?

Max Lucado, Max; It's Not About Me; (Nashville, TN; Integrity, 2004) Pg. 6

Chapter 3

Wait and See

Entering Mayo Clinic gives one a sense of wonderment. The massive hallways and marble-like floors display themselves with spotless sheen. Signs giving directions hang in plain view accompanied by courteous volunteers eager to give further guidance if needed. Inter-department communication and schedules reflect the utmost organization of the entire clinic.

With my appointment itinerary in hand, Burt and I made our way to the lab. Several vials of blood were drawn. Next, we went to the imaging department for a full-body CT scan. I was done by mid-morning, but my appointment with the oncologist was not until early afternoon, so Burt and I enjoyed a leisure breakfast at a restaurant and explored a little of Rochester before returning to the clinic to meet with the oncologist.

We stepped off the elevator on the tenth floor of Mayo Clinic. Many people sat in the large waiting area of the oncology department. Magazine tables placed strategically amongst the seating gave the appearance of cozy conversational areas. As I looked from face to face, I sensed some, like me, were here for the first time. I noticed some acted nervous. Others chatted pleasantly with those that sat nearby—their topics of conversation centered mostly on where they lived and little about their cancer. A few sat in chairs on the far side near the windows huddled in a blanket with a scarf or hat covering their heads—obviously feeling ill. Each face had their own story of their journey through the valley of the shadow of death. But they were more than faces—they were human beings with feelings and fears and hopes. Like me.

O how I wanted to wrap my arms about them; to give what comfort I could, but that may have been an unwanted intrusion into their space, so I simply waited for my name to be called.

After a few minutes, I heard, "Rita Kroon to door B." Burt and I were led to a small consultation room. We sat down. My palms felt sweaty, and my stomach jittered. Burt seemed calm as he and I made small talk.

"Sure is nice to get the results the same day the tests are done," Burt said.

"Yes, for sure," I replied.

Then Dr. Marks entered. He greeted us warmly and sat at a small computer desk next to where I sat. He had a Tom Selleck mustache and eyes that seemed to take in more than the obvious. His demeanor had a calming effect.

We talked in length about my surgery three months prior and my hesitation to proceed with radiation.

"I think you did the right thing at this juncture," he said. "We know the GYN surgeon left a margin of cancer so we will do a wait-and-see. We know the what and we know the where of the cancer, but we don't know the when."

I breathed in deeply and let it out slowly.

He turned the monitor screen towards us so we could see. "In the meantime," Dr. Marks said, "the CT shows a spot on your lower right lung that is a little worrisome."

Words from a long-forgotten source flashed through my mind. "God directs my steps as well as my stops." *O dear God, I can't do this. Give me strength.*

"Let's schedule you for a return check in November for a CT and see what we're dealing with."

Not at all what I expected to hear!

Chapter 4

Tragedy Strikes

On October 27, 2004, at 5:00 p.m. my phone rang. My sister-in-law spoke with words choked by sobs. "Rob - was killed - in a truck accident," she wailed.

I crumpled onto a chair at our kitchen table. I could not speak as sobs heaved my chest. My lungs felt like they were about to cave in. "How?" I finally managed to ask.

"A truck traveling the opposite direction—the driver lost control—crossed the median right in front of Rob's truck." More sobs. "His truck burned." Then she said, "It was instant."

My mind swirled with disbelief. I felt dizzy. My heart pounded in my ears. "Where?" I asked.

"Just outside of Rochester."

After more weeping and sobbing, unable to console each other, we hung up. I sat there and sobbed at the death of my brother—my brother, who handed the baton to his co-worker who handed it to his sister in Florida who emailed me suggesting I go to Rochester for a second opinion.

Burt tried to comfort me, but he could not soften the shock of it. We drove to the assisted living/memory care center where I had recently placed my eighty-six-year-old mother. Because she was in the mid stages of Alzheimer's disease, I was not certain she would be able to completely grasp the unthinkable news I had to tell her.

"Mom." I had to stop and collect my thoughts. "You know Rob drives a big rig, right?"

She nodded.

"Today he had an accident."

Her eyes widened with a look of alarm and worry.

I looked away brushing tears from my cheeks. I tried to speak these stinging words as soothingly as possible. I choked on my own sobs. "Mom, he didn't make it."

She stared at me. Her eyes filled with tears. "Rob is gone?"

"Yes, Mom," I answered, hugging her. I felt a deep pain for her. Her oldest son—her first-born was gone. I looked at my frail mother trying to grasp the enormity of my words. "But Rob is in heaven with Jesus and Dad and Davey," I offered.

She brightened slightly, but then her tears would come again. And so did mine.

I thought about my dad who died of cancer in 1971, my younger brother, Dave, who at age 18 died of muscular dystrophy in 1969, my aging mother with Alzheimer's disease, and now my older brother killed in a truck accident. And I have cancer. All that was left of my extended family was my younger sister and me. At that moment it was nearly impossible for me to be comforted with words I knew to be true in my head, but I could not get my heart to reconcile with them in my grief.

I knew the heavenly Father lost His only begotten Son on the cross. He understood the pain of losing a Son. Because of His hate for sin and His love for us, Jesus died in our place. He rose victorious over death, and that He gives eternal life to all who believe in Him, and death shall be no more. Jesus trampled over death with death. I felt comforted because we have hope.

I took Mom's Bible from her small nightstand and turned to Revelation 21:4. "God Himself will wipe away our tears and there will be no more mourning, or crying, or pain anymore for the former things have passed away." I began to focus on His promises, and as I did so, I felt His soothing balm wash over me with glorious relief.

Mom slipped back into her dark world of confusion. "I don't know where I'm supposed to be."
I just hugged her. Burt hugged her.

By November 6, my brother's funeral was over, out-of-town guests were gone, thank-you notes had been written, and the flowers faded. And the clock keeps ticking.

An election has been won, routines were reinstated, leaves continued to fall. And time marches each of us to our destiny.

Sometime later, I listened to Chuck Swindoll speak on the radio. He talked about tragedies that happen—for example, the death of a loved one. I perked up as he seemed to be speaking directly to me. Swindoll made a statement that caused me to think from a different perspective.

He said, "When we don't understand why something has happened, listen to what Jesus might be saying: 'Can you thank Me for trusting you with this experience even though I may not tell you why?'"

Difficult and thought-provoking, I thought. I turned his words over in my mind again and again. *Hard to grasp, but necessary for healing of the heart.*

Swindoll went on to say that God has a purpose and will work out all things for good to those who love Him. We are assured that our prayers do make a difference—not because of who we are or what we say, but because of who God is. Swindoll concluded by saying that the power of prayer does not lie in the one who speaks, but in the One who hears.

Chapter 5

Angel in Disguise

By the time mid-November arrived, my scheduled appointment at Mayo Clinic shifted my attention from grief at the loss of my brother to the immediacy of my medical situation. The blood work, CT, and meeting with the oncologist repeated itself with less fear of an unknown routine than the previous appointment three months prior. However, I held much apprehension for the spot on my lung.

Once again Dr. Marks turned the computer monitor towards us as Burt and I tried to decipher the images on the screen. "The nodule in your lower right lung is unchanged," Dr. Marks said.

I felt relief begin to surge until he continued, "So, we will pursue this."

"But I thought if there was no change, that was a good sign," I said.

"Not always," he countered. "A PET scan will be a little more helpful in accurately diagnosing this. If there is any cancer, those areas will light up."

It was late November, when Burt and I drove the eighty-five miles back to Rochester for the PET scan. I sat in an easy-type chair in a room with soft music and dimmed lights while Burt waited in the waiting room. I was to relax and sit perfectly motionless for forty-five minutes. I would then be placed in a tube for the PET scan.

But, a few minutes after being injected with radio-active sugar water, my heart began to race. I couldn't even count the beats. I pressed the nurse-call button, moving only my finger.

She came, took my pulse, and immediately called the heart doctor.

I was hooked up to a heart monitor.

"Your heart is beating fast, but it's regular," the doctor said. "You must have reacted to the sugar."

"I have hypoglycemia," I mumbled, trying to remain still.

"We'll continue to monitor you. Please, try not to move."

Breathing was difficult, but having to remain still was nearly impossible.

After forty-five minutes, my arms were strapped across my chest and a band across my forehead prior to going into the tube to complete the PET scan. My anxiety at being constrained, my racing heart and the claustrophobia in the tube nearly did me in. When it was over, I felt weak and shaky, but still alive.

Burt and I met with Dr. Marks later that day.

"The spot in your lung lit up." He paused briefly before continuing. "And your adrenal glands lit up as well," he finished in a solemn tone.

When peace flees like a dove to a far-off land, pray for me, I whispered in my soul.

"We'll schedule you for a biopsy of the adrenal glands before we proceed further."

I could not speak. I could hardly breathe. I felt numb.

"What are adrenal glands?" It was Burt who asked.

"They are the glands that sit right above the kidneys. They're part of the endocrine system, and their main function is the release of hormones associated with stress."

"Mine sure have had a workout!" I said, trying to join their conversation and the world of reality.

He nodded with a slight smile.

A few days later in early December, I had the biopsy done on the adrenal glands, and then we met with Dr. Marks for the results.

"There is no cancer in the adrenal glands," he said. "And that is a good thing because if you had cancer of the adrenal glands, that would have complicated matters tremendously."

"But I thought the PET scan lit up," I said.

"They lit up differently than the spot on your lung, but we wanted to make certain— hence the biopsy."

After further discussion regarding my spot on my lung, surgery was scheduled for December 16 with a lung surgery specialist.

"I realize you will be having another major surgery barely five months after your first surgery for leiomyosarcoma," Dr. Marks said, "but I think we need to move on this."

His demeanor did not portray any alarm—only an unassuming calmness that settled my anxiety to a tolerable level.

Christmas shopping and decorating became a good diversion to the pending lung surgery, although I think I made much of the festive preparations so that this would be the best Christmas ever! I wanted everything finished so that when I returned home from the hospital, our family could enjoy Christmas without any last minute primping.

I also reflected on the real meaning of Christmas—how God came in the flesh to be our Savior. I wondered if God was even pleased with my feeble and inept way of celebrating the birth of His Son. Strangely, my Christmas readying and even my pending surgery paled in significance of that miracle. God became man.

It was at this time that our eleven-year old grandson seemed to have a particularly tough time with my upcoming surgery. "Ryan, are you okay with everything?" I asked over the phone.

"Yeah," he mumbled

"You know Gramma is having surgery on Thursday," I continued.

"I know," he answered, barely above a whisper.

"Well, do you know what I did?" I could picture the sullen look on his face as he answered, "What?"

"I invited Jesus into the operating room with me."

"Yeah, but you can't see Him."

"No, I can't, but I know He will be there with me," I said. "I can't see you either, but I know you are there. It's the same with Jesus."

The morning of my lung surgery brought our three married daughters to St. Mary's Hospital in Rochester to be with Burt and me. LaDawn, Rene´, and Shelly prayed with us. *Wouldn't it be awesome,* I thought, *if we could look up from prayer and see Jesus listening?* But I knew He was. We hugged, and we wept. I did not think of the weeping as a lack of faith as much as an emotion most human beings express to one another prior to surgery—ours was no exception.

As the nurse wheeled my bed out into the hallway, she stopped momentarily as I waved to our three daughters and received teary smiles and thumbs' up from them.

It was then that I then noticed a man wearing a suit and tie standing directly across the hall from me. This impeccably dressed man and I made eye contact. He smiled as he approached me. He held a small, plain wooden cross in his hand and offered it to me saying, "I thought you might like to have this."

I took the cross from the kind stranger, and then he was gone. Neither the nurse, nor Burt nor I said anything. We simply went on our way down the hallway to surgery as though this were not a most astonishing thing!

While Burt and I waited in the pre-op area, another nurse sitting at a desk noticed the cross I held and came over to us. "May I pray with you?" she asked with a gentle voice.

"Of course," Burt and I said in unison. We joined hands as she prayed that God would keep His hand upon me and that my surgery would go well.

How awesome that the Lord would give me a tangible sign—something that I could hold—that He was with me and that He would never leave me. The words I first prayed at the beginning of this journey came to mind. "Dear Lord, please show me Your presence in such a way that I will know for certain that You are with me."

"Thank You too, for this nurse," I whispered as I was wheeled into surgery.

My surgery lasted five hours. When I recovered sufficiently, I noticed a drainage tube on my lower right side. *Well, that certainly is gross.*

Later, I was moved to my hospital room. The lung surgeon and his team entered. He explained that the drainage tube was necessary because there was a spot in the lining of my lung that remained open and that the other end of the tube was up near my collar bone. I was told that I would have to wear surgical scissors on a cord around my neck twenty-four hours a day for the next two weeks in case the tube kinked. If that happened, I was to cut the cord immediately to prevent my lung from collapsing. That gave me an extremely uneasy feeling. I hardly dared to move, and the pain was so great that I did not want to move.

"You had a tumor the size of a pencil eraser in the lower lobe of your lung. We did a thoracotomy lobectomy which means that we took the lower right lobe of your lung," the surgeon explained.

"Was it cancer?" I asked.

"It appears to be cancer, but we won't know for sure what kind of cancer until we get the results from pathology. We'll talk more about that at your follow-up visit in a couple of weeks."

While I was still processing the fact that I have had my second major surgery for cancer in five months, I heard soft cries from my roommate on the other side of the curtain. I asked Burt to pull back the curtain enough that I could see a woman who appeared to be in her mid-fifties.

"I do not want to intrude," I began, "but if you would like to talk, I would like to listen."

She looked at me with frightened eyes. "I just had a biopsy done on one of several nodules that are in both of my lungs," she cried.

I nodded and understanding nod.

"My leiomyosarcoma has spread to my lungs," she blurted.

"Leiomyosarcoma?" I asked. I began to tremble.

"Yeah, it's a rare cancer that she's got." The voice was that of a man who sat in a chair next to her bed. "I'm Chuck and this here is Norma," he said.

"I'm Rita and this is my husband Burt," I said, as I realized that now I knew three of the four in a million who have leiomyosarcoma.

Burt and I tried to encourage this couple to trust in Jesus for whatever the outcome, but then our brief conversation was interrupted when our three daughters entered the room.

Norma was discharged the next day to await her upcoming surgery. Before Chuck packed up her belongings, I had another opportunity to talk to her about the Lord.

"I don't know why I didn't think about God before," she confessed, and the door to the throne room of God Almighty opened.
Our visit with our daughters was solemn, but not without hope.

Our Christmas celebration seemed almost as obscure as the small town of Bethlehem where the Christ child was born. I was not up to much of the festivities due to the intense pain of recovering from lung surgery. The surgeon had to crack two of my ribs to do the lobectomy.

My days until my two-week check-up filled themselves with times of feeling down interspersed with wonderful times of uplifting gratitude for my many blessings. My husband still calls me his beautiful bride and greets me with gentle hugs and tender kisses. Our three married daughters and their precious families stopped by often.

My sister, Gayle, moved back from New York not only to be near, but to help care for our mother who was advancing in her Alzheimer's disease.

My wonderful church family and thoughtful neighbors brought prepared meals and cards of encouragement. I had prayer warriors across the nation show incredible support for me by their passionate prayers and their tangible expressions of love.

The two weeks to my follow-up appointment passed without incident, and I was much relieved that I did not have to use the scissors that dangled around my neck. The drainage tube was removed painlessly and easily. Then the lung surgeon entered the room.

"The tumor we removed was indeed cancer— bronchioloalveolar carcinoma which means a non-smoker's, small cell cancer," he said. "That is a different form of cancer than your leiomyosarcoma, and that is a good thing."

"Do you mean that I have two different kinds of cancer in my body at the same time? How is that a good thing?" I asked, trying to understand how this could be possible. *It's not about me;* I had to remind myself silently. *It's not about me.*

Burt squeezed my hand as though to prepare me for the worst.

"It is a good thing because that means your first cancer has not spread." He reassured me that he had gotten the entire tumor and left no margin of cancer. Therefore, no further treatment was necessary. After the meeting with the surgeon, we met with Dr. Marks, the oncologist.

"We'll continue to monitor you for leiomyosarcoma," he said. "We'll see you in early April for another CT of your abdomen."

This day, my faith has been tested. My endurance has been reached. I was discouraged and my faith began to waver with the long and painful recovery from lung surgery. Despair and depression waited to be introduced to me as though they would be my constant companions.

At the same time, I happened to read the Biblical account found in Mark 4 of several fishermen in a boat with Jesus asleep on a cushion in the stern. A violent storm arose on the lake and the disciples were terrified that they would die.

Jesus was right there with them in the boat albeit asleep, but He was there with them. The men cried out to Him to save them. The Lord arose and rebuked the wind. And the sea became calm. Jesus chided them tenderly for their little faith. But did He abandon them? Of course not, I reminded myself.

I read again that the disciples marveled saying, "Who is this, that even the wind and the sea obey Him?"

Did Jesus love them any less because of their little faith? Of course not, I thought with surety. I believe that Jesus is faithful, sovereign, and compassionate and the epitome of love, and how we respond to circumstances around us does in no way alter His character or His love for us.

Jesus came to the fishermen's rescue. He also came to mine. A huge wave was about to capsize my boat, but once again, I glimpsed the incredible, immeasurable love of Jesus.

He didn't silently slip encouragement and hope into my soul. No, He sent food. Six of our neighbor ladies each brought over a complete meal—all prepared, wrapped for freezing, and labeled with instructions for heating.

I failed my test of faith, but His faithfulness never fails.

Chapter 6

The Unforeseen Enemy

I flipped through the February issue of Daily Bread and read, "Every difficult circumstance is timed with exact precision. Every hard situation is screened through His perfect love."

I had to ponder that for a bit before I concluded that my cancer was not a random thing. God ordained it through His perfect love for my spiritual good. Those who realize they are being tested by fire are those who manage to keep an eye on heaven while walking through the valley of the shadow of death. There are times, however, that I fear I may have HADD— Heaven Attention Deficit Disorder.

April, 2005, brought good results from my blood work and CT scan. However, in May, I again experienced a cramping feeling in my lower abdomen and a mild temperature. I met with my primary doctor and was told that my white count was elevated. My doctor thought it best I return to the oncologist at Mayo Clinic.

Catherine Marshall said, "God sees to it that sight never precedes faith." I am like one peeking under the curtain of a dark stage.

On May 10, I had more blood work and another CT at Mayo Clinic.

Dr. Marks said, "There is a small spot in the same area of your previous leiomyosarcoma. It looks like it could be a fluid sac, but we'll keep an eye on it. We'll scan you again in August."

At this point and if I had foresight, I would have played the theme music from the movie "Jaws." However, I did not have such luxury, so I simply delighted to spend the spring working in my rock garden in our back yard and to spend most weekends at our cabin.

One beautiful day late in May, I tried to capture the essence of the prelude to summer by writing this poem:

"Spring"

Spring is a dance
of the season;
Winter bows its head –
Summer applauds;
Autumn waits patiently.

Life raises its head
and is reborn;
Breath ebbs and flows
Creating the breeze;
The heart begins to beat.

Colors burst forth
in profusion;
Fragrances mingle
In harmony;
The earth sings a new song.

The Conductor raises
His baton;
The orchestra plays
in unison;
Spring dances to the melody.

While at the cabin, Burt challenged our daughter, René, to see who could read more pages in a book. Her husband, Brian, went fishing. And I walked along the gravel road searching for agates with those grandkids too young to go four-wheeling. We all delighted to watch fingers of orange spread across the early morning sky long before swimming or skipping rocks across the Kettle River became a realization.

On those nights that it rained, we would turn off the lights in the cabin and tell scary stories. All through summer, I felt fine. And yet, thoughts a possible return of the cancer played hide 'n' seek in my mind. The CT scan on August 16 "showed no significant findings," even though I had begun to have moderate, but sporadic pain, in my lower left abdomen area throughout the week. I was troubled that I would have such symptoms and yet, have no significant findings on the CT.

The next day brought unrelenting pain with additional pain in my left leg and into my lower back. I called Mayo Clinic but was reassured my CT was clear and did not warrant a visit to the clinic.

On August 18, I saw my primary doctor. He did a urinalysis and blood work, but nothing showed up. "All seems fine. I am stumped," he said.

As the summer season wound down and we settled into September, I was reminded to set my mind on the things above, not on things that are on earth. (Colossians 3:2) I do not want to stumble along with my eyes to the ground when I should be focused on Christ.

The autumn leaves displayed their glorious colors and then drifted to earth giving only the allusion of the life they once held as they turned brown and lay on the ground. It was November.

An intense, gnawing pain in my lower left abdomen gripped me relentlessly. My temperature stayed at 100 degrees. I did not feel well. Burt thought it best to go to the ER at St. Mary's Hospital in Rochester.

A thought in the form of a question came to mind as we drove to Rochester. *Would I rather be tempted by Satan or tested by fire?* At first, I reasoned that it would be easier to resist the devil than to go through a difficult and unpleasant trial by the Lord. But then, I realized that I would rather be in the hands of God than in the crosshairs of Satan.

Once at the hospital, they did blood work, urinalysis, and a CT scan. The attractive female doctor told me that the scan showed a tumor in the same area as my first cancer surgery and I was to call my oncologist, Dr. Marks, on Monday. My cancer was back!

But I was not abandoned in the ER room. The nurse who disconnected the IV gave me a paper cup of cool water to drink and said, "I wish I could give you more than a cup of water—like prayers," she said.

"You can," I answered. She smiled and I knew she would.

I know prayer is a vital part of every believer's faith, but could it be that our prayers are conditioned upon God's purpose? That our prayers are bound by His will for His glory and not the other way around?

I took delight when the man who transported me back from the CT said, "God bless you."

I prayed too. "Heavenly Father, You are the Lord of the heavens and the earth. Thank You for placing me in the presence of other believers. It is such a confirmation that You are with me. I know you will not abandon me. Help me to remember that I am not on the battlefield alone. In Jesus' Name I pray."

"Every journey begins with one step." These timely and fitting words splashed across a card I had received sometime earlier came rushing to mind. The words were superimposed over the word 'hope'. I lingered on that message as further encouragement from the Lord.

On the following Monday, Burt and I sat with the oncologist. Dr. Marks looked at the scan images on the monitor. He shook his head slowly and said, "Leiomyosarcoma is an elusive and persistent cancer. Your cancer is definitely back." He arranged for me to meet with him, Dr. Dozois (colorectal surgeon), a radiologist, and a GYN.

By the end of November, Dr. Marks informed me that Dr. Dozois was putting a team together for what they anticipated would be a very difficult surgery. I had a

PAP smear and while the female GYN and I talked together, I told her about my hesitation to have radiation. She told me of her own breast cancer and her reluctance to have radiation as well.

 "But that is a decision each person must make on their own," she said sympathetically.

Then we met with Dr. Ivy Petersen, a radiation oncologist. She was kind, gentle, and understanding. She thoroughly explained the purpose of radiation and the necessity for it in certain cancerous situations.

Bouts of anxiety and sheer panic traded places frequently with peace and hope. I felt like I was in a hurricane being tossed every which way. I shed many tears at the thought of another surgery—tears for my family and the stress this put on each of them. I could not see any way to get around these seemingly insurmountable roadblocks. O how I did not want to venture forward to what lay before me.

 I prayed with our daughter, Shelly. Because Shelly and her husband and their four children lived in Iowa, we did most of our praying over the phone. Together we cast our cares, burdens, and anxieties on Him—the One who cares for us as 1 Peter 5:7 says.

"You cannot trust in man, or man's technology, or man's wisdom, but you can trust that God is working through His chosen agents on your behalf," Shelly said. I again felt the peace of God begin to soothe my soul.

Did not David say in Psalm 56:8, "O God, You have put my tears in Your bottle?" *Are You, O God, not attentive to every detail of my life as well?*

We decided that I would not have radiation and would proceed with surgery.

By mid-December, several teams of surgeons were coordinated. Urology and vascular were added to those already in place. The surgery was set for December 30, 2005.

The pastor at our Church where we attend spoke about God's sustaining grace. "The grace that orders our pain is the same grace that sustains us in darkness." I thought on those words throughout the Christmas season.

We celebrated Christmas at our home as usual. Decorations, meals, and gifts took on a rather simplistic nature as we all focused on the birth of Christ and the importance of close-knit family relationships.

I filled my time from Christmas to surgery reading God's Word and drinking deeply of its truths. I read James 1:2-3. "Count it all joy, my brethren, when you meet trials of various kinds, for you know that the testing of your faith produces steadfastness." (ESV) I contemplated life on earth. I pondered eternal life. O how I delighted in knowing that salvation was not appropriated by the lowest bidder. On the contrary, salvation was made sure by the One who paid the highest price! Again, I was encouraged to know how precious we are in the sight of the Lord.

I thought about the peace that passes all understanding that will keep our hearts and minds in Christ Jesus. (Philippians 4:7) How easy to be still when pleasant situations abound. But peace must be more than comfortable circumstances, I reasoned to myself. I concluded that peace is the complete acceptance of God's total grace in *any* given situation. Psalm 46:10 says, "Be still and know that I am God." Contentment results from an inner satisfaction with the situation that God has ordained for each of us.

When I struggle with not being content in my circumstances, I chide myself that I'm thinking that it's still all about me. And I pray for the Lord to change my focus.

And yet, anxiety, that relentless, uninvited enemy, bulldozes its way in, crowds out peace, and extinguishes joy. It gets worse when anxiety's ugly roommate, fear, swoops in and caters only to itself without care for the destruction it causes.

"Lord, help me to cast off fear and anxiety and put on the full armor of God," I whispered. I knew my faith needed a major strengthening if it was to sustain me on the battlefield.

Surgery day came all too quickly. Once again, my husband and our three married daughters made a circle about me. LaDawn led us in prayer asking that I be protected, and that the Father's will be done.

I knew our sons-in-law did the same while on their jobs. Our grandkids each made precious cards and sent them with our daughters so that I would see them as soon as I returned to my room after surgery.

I looked forward to seeing my sons-in-law and my grandkids as I knew they were eager to come see me too.

Chapter 7

The Other Side of Hope

Surgery lasted nine hours and I was told it proved to be more complicated than originally anticipated.

"During surgery, she lost six units of blood and had to be transfused," Dr. Dozois explained to my family in the family waiting room while I remained in ICU. "But the good news is there is no margin of cancer."

Early in the evening after surgery, I developed a large blood clot in my upper left leg. I had a lot of swelling and it felt like my leg and foot were about to explode. My leg was wrapped in towels and I was taken to surgery to have an IVC filter placed at the base of my aorta to prevent the clot from going to my heart or lungs. I was put on heparin administered by shots in the abdomen to try to dissolve the clot and avoid surgery.

My blood got too thin, so I had to be given vitamin K. Twice I had to be given platelets and more blood to get my hemoglobin up.

I had much swelling throughout my whole body from fluid retention and was given Lasix, but then I had to be given potassium when the fluid loss was too rapid. Around 11:00 p.m., I experienced great difficulty in breathing so I was given another CT to see why. I was relieved to find out that it was not a blood clot, but rather fluid in and around my lungs. "The Lasix should help," I was told.

Because of the many serious complications post-op, my family members who were not with me prior to surgery were told to wait a few days before coming to visit me.

On the fifth night after surgery while still in ICU, I awoke at around 1:30 a.m. I loathed the rhythmic sound of the suction machine plugged into the wall that pumped extra fluids from my incision in my abdomen. The pump to keep circulation in my leg compressed and released, compressed, and released as though the pump itself mocked me as it seemed to expel air and gasp for more. I looked at all the IV tubes that hung like a maze of tangled mass—drip, drip, drip.

I felt alert in my thinking in the darkened hospital room illumined only by the soft light in the hallway. A strange depression began to creep over me—slowly and subtly at first. How strange, I thought, that I did not try to stop the downward spiral that brought me to a dark place I had never known to exist. It was as though I had instantly analyzed the process and accepted a fateful outcome. I was tumbling into darkness. I had lost all hope. I thought about my husband; nothing. I thought about our three daughters and their husbands; only detachment. I thought about our grandchildren as though they were complete strangers. I felt totally disconnected from everything and everyone that was important to me—the ones who always put a smile on my face and joy in my heart.

Even thinking about God did not matter. Prayer to escape this dark world was the furthest thing from my mind. I could not pray. I did not care enough to pray. I laid there with tears slipping down my face. If this was the tunnel of death, I accepted it without struggle. Darkness swirled around me. I didn't care.

It would have taken the expending of more energy to fight the enemy of despair than to seek God's presence, but I had no strength or will for either, and so I sank in the mire.

A nurse entered my room. "Are you all right, Mrs. Kroon?" she asked.

"Yes," I answered.

"Would you like something to help you sleep?"

"No," I said, simply.

The nurse stopped in to check on me several times throughout the night. She was pleasant enough and seemed to want to stay, but I only answered what she asked and then would watch her slip out of my semi-dark room. It was as though I was watching with detachment a formless shadow slip into the light of the hallway.

The enemy's lie had entered my mind in a whisper in the night.

I came to the conclusion that if I did not die in the hospital I would go home and let Hospice do whatever they do. I told the nurse of my decision on one of her visits to my room.

She raised her eyebrows slightly, nodded, and rubbed my hand in a way that said she understood.

I would await death without fear or dread.

Early in the morning, the surgical team arrived on their rounds. After asking how I was doing, I spoke matter-of-factly to the surgeon as I relayed my intention to go home. Unbeknownst to me at the time, however, was that the night nurse had told Dr. Dozois I had given up all hope and had sunk into deep despair.

"Do you know what we're going to do?" he asked with a broad grin. Without waiting for my reply, he continued, "We are going to move you to a real hospital room with a window. We're going to get you some real food, and we're going to get you up out of bed today."

It was a good thing he had enough enthusiasm for both of us since I did not share in his optimism one iota. I'm certain the expression on my face said it all.

I'm living proof of Proverbs 13:12 "Hope deferred makes the heart sick, but a desire filled makes a tree of life."

Within two hours, however, I was looking out a window on the first floor. I saw people and cars and buses. I noticed the slushy streets on that clear January morning. The coffee shop across the street bustled as people entered and exited carrying paper cups of coffee and sacks of bagels. I could almost smell the aroma of the steaming coffee.

The sound of the suction pump and the leg compression pump retreated into a muffled silence.

Hope began to trickle into my soul.

A tray was brought into my room and placed on my movable serving table. The nurse propped up my pillow and turned the tray towards me. She lifted the cover and there sat the most beautiful sight I had ever seen—orange jello.

I smiled ever so slightly as the words of Matthew 28:20 came to mind. Jesus said, "I am with you always; even to the end of the age."

I recognized that what I had experienced the night before was not that Jesus had abandoned me, but that I had lost my awareness of Him which led me to ponder a question that I put to myself: How did I not recognize Satan's attack, and why did I become such easy prey?

I should have cried out to the Lord, "Help me. I need you, Jesus. I can't do this. It's too overwhelming." Instead, I surrendered to the darkness. I felt myself slip further and further down into hopelessness. I did not care how deep into despair I had traveled. I felt totally alone.

I turned my attention to the nourishment set before me. I savored the jello as I reached for the Bible in the drawer of the bedside stand. I turned to Psalms. "Why are you in despair, O my soul? And why have you become disturbed within me? Hope in God, for I shall yet praise Him, the help of my countenance, and my God." The psalmist's words described my despair exactly, and his words of encouragement lifted my spirit. (Psalm 42:11)

Hope began to surge into my soul like crude oil does in a newly tapped well. I began to feel as though I wanted to get back to a world where people lived and breathed and greeted one another.

By mid-morning, several vases of flowers that were not permitted in ICU arrived. The sweet fragrance of the many flowers filled the room. As I breathed in deeply, I closed my eyes. I could almost imagine myself being in a garden. I was reminded of another garden, Gethsemane, and how the sacrifice of Jesus for all mankind must have been a sweet fragrance to the Father.

"Thank You, Father, for the fragrance of flowers as a reminder of the sweet aroma of Jesus Christ for my sake," I whispered as Burt entered my room.

Chapter 8

The Calm before the Storm

"**Y**ou look like you're having fun smiling," Burt greeted.

"I am and let me tell you why," I answered. I told Burt about the darkness I had plunged into the night before, and how the Lord worked through Dr. Dozois to move me back to the 'land of the living.'

Even though I still had the IV's and the leg compression pump on an off-and-on basis, I reveled in the freedom from the suction pump draining my abdomen. I could get out of bed and walk without waiting for someone to detach me from the wall. And the more I walked, the less I had to have the compression leg pump. I just knew recovery would go quickly.

For God alone, O my soul, wait in silence, for my hope is from Him. Psalm 62:5

I nearly squealed with delight when LaDawn and Mike and their two children, Ryan and Faith, came to visit followed by René and Brian and their two sons, Michael and Jesse.

"I should have baked a cake or something," I said as they crowded into my cluttered space.

"Yeah, Gramma, where's the cake?" fourteen-year old Michael asked.

"You could've at least had some chocolate chip cookies," eleven-year old Ryan chimed in.

"Candy!" Jesse said. "People in hospitals always have a box of candy somewhere, and you know thirteen-year olds always want candy."

I looked at Burt who simply shrugged.

"I brought you some candy," seven-year old Faith said softly and held out a box of miniature turtles.

"Thank you, sweetie," I said, giving her a hug. "Would you pass them around?"

It became a joke with my family to tease me about having sweets around since I loved to bake, but I, myself, had not eaten sugar for almost thirty years.

Even though our other daughter, Shelly was expecting their fifth baby in less than a week, she and Scott drove from Iowa the following day along with their four children.

Ten-year-old Kari hopped up on my bed and snuggled next to me as though I was dressed in lounging pajamas and resting in the comforts of a luxury bed. Eight year old Tony, six year old Jacob, and two year old Rachel gave me delicate hugs as though not wanting to hurt me. For the most part, they seemed content to look with wide eyes around the room.

January 8, 2006, Burt accompanied me as the nurse wheeled me to the lobby door. A young man followed us pushing a cart loaded with flowers and cards. The cold air stung my cheeks, but I did not mind it at all. We were heading home!

René and I talked on that cold, January day. "I feel disappointed in my Christian walk," she said.

"Why is that?" I asked with concern.

"Because if something would have happened to you during surgery, I don't think I would have been able to praise God. It's only because surgery was successful that I can give praise to the Lord."

"You know, Rene´, I thought I had a strong faith prior to cancer," I spoke, "but then life was good and comfortable and pleasant. I was in a good season. But, when trials make life uncertain, even painful, and challenging, I realized that I needed a work done within me," I said.

"Why do you think that happens?' she asked.

"It seems to me that God compels us to stop and take a long hard look at where we are in our walk of faith. I have had to do the same over these past few years; sometimes confidently and trusting; other times filled with fear and dread, but always knowing He is working in my life for my good."

"So, were you ever disappointed with your lack of faith?" René pressed.

"Of course. But we all need these check points—not as a stopping place to be discouraged, but rather as a springboard to persevere in faith with renewed commitment," I said. "Reminds me of something Max Lucado said, 'Your eyes see your faults; your faith sees your Savior.'"

"So, it's okay to be discontent during those times we have a lack of faith?"

"Absolutely. I think it's better to be aware of those times of little faith than to not recognize them at all," I replied.

"So, it's like a growing process then?" she asked.

"Exactly." I nodded. "And sometimes, it may take a long time."

"Do you think God is pleased when we ask Him to give us faith to believe in all situations?"

"He will not deny us."

By mid-January, the catheter was removed. I still had much swelling in my leg, but walking and lying down with my leg elevated helped. Coumadin for anticoagulation management held the INR in check, so the possibility of having another blood clot seemed a little more remote. Although to stay on the blood thinner for a whole year was more than I bargained for.

The end of January, I developed a bladder infection; "probably from the stint that was placed in the ureter tube," the doctor said. Then in early February I developed cellulite of the anterior abdominal wall along both sides of the incision. Antibiotics were administered and cleared the infections and the stint was removed without complications. It was like a couple of hiccups in comparison to the three major surgeries in less than two years.

I was well on my way to recovery until April which brought a bout of pneumonia, but that too was easily treated. I considered it a small hurdle and looked forward to the coming summer.

I went to Mayo Clinic for my scheduled CT the end of July, 2006. Dr. Dozois informed me that an indeterminate spot appeared in my lower abdomen and that I was to meet with Dr. Marks, my oncologist, in a couple of days. I was devastated beyond words even though Dr. Marks thought it to be benign, "but we will watch it," he said. Another follow-up CT scan and a MRI were to be done the end of September.

After the MRI and while on our way to other doctors' appointments, Burt told me that while I was in the MRI tube, and as he stood at my head, he prayed. "Lord, I'm worried about my wife. How can I support her and pray for her?"

"Immediately these words came to mind," he said. 'Do not worry. She belongs to Me.' "I wasn't sure if that was my own thinking or from the Lord, so I prayed again," Burt said. "Lord, how can I help my wife? Will she be all right?"

Again, he said these words came to him: 'Do not worry. She will be all right. She is mine.' Burt said he was much comforted and encouraged.

My hope soared, and I felt strengthened to face whatever adversity may lie ahead. My Savior knew me, and I was in His care.

Both Dr. Marks and Dr. Dozois agreed that the spot has not changed so they will continue to monitor.

Lewis Smedes once said, "Waiting is the hardest work of hope." I agree.

I became weary with all the tests and procedures and with the nagging thought that my leiomyosarcoma might be back for the third time.

O how I desired to have thoughts that were not tainted with the possibility of cancer. I pushed myself to focus on the fact that life is not about me; it is about God and that He loves me, not for who I am or for what I do, but because it is His nature to love. I know I can trust the God of love as I wait for Him to heal me or to strengthen me for yet another battle.

I know that God can heal me; I don't know if He will, but even if He doesn't, I still know that He can.

Another Christmas passed with special family celebrations, decorations, baked goods, and gifts. And yet, a smudge seemed to mar the festivities as my dread of the results of my CT scan scheduled for early February simmered like a pot on a back burner.

Chapter 9

Valley of the Shadow of Death

I entered 2007 with much apprehension for I could think of little else except what might lie ahead. My February 14th appointment arrived all too quickly. After my CT scan, Burt and I met with Dr. Marks. "The spot we were watching has grown to about one inch which is a little larger than the tumor you had in your surgery of December, 2005."

This was sweetheart's day—a time to celebrate love; not a day to hear such dire news!

I could not even speak as tears stung my eyes. Burt squeezed my hand as though to protect me from the sting of the news. The words were said. There was no taking them back.

"Lord Jesus, help me know You are with me. Help me to persevere," I whispered in desperate prayer.

"I think we need to talk about radiation prior to surgery," Dr. Marks said in a serious tone. I looked intently at my oncologist. *I don't want to be here. I don't want to go through this.* My mind defied reality. My body felt numb.

"I'll set up an appointment with Dr. Petersen, the radiation oncologist, and with Dr. Dozois for the coming week."

It was Burt who spoke. "What is involved with radiation?"

"My thought would be twenty five treatments over a five week period and probably some intra-operative radiation as well. But I don't want to get ahead of myself," Dr. Marks said cautiously, "so I would like you to meet with Dr. Petersen and she will be able to better plan the course of treatment that's best suited for your needs."

Dr. Dozois, colorectal surgeon, agreed with Dr. Marks that I needed to have radiation prior to surgery. "It is imperative that you have radiation prior to surgery in order to have intra-operative radiation which, I think, is your only option at this point." And then he added, "And that is not even a guarantee. We are dealing with a very persistent and angry cancer, but it boosts your chance for survival over not having the radiation."

"What are my odds of survival?" I asked.

"About fifty-fifty," they said.

"Fifty-fifty?" My shoulders slumped.

"Those are good odds from a doctor's standpoint," they assured me.

I took in a deep breath and let it out slowly. "Okay," I agreed. I trusted Dr. Dozois' urging. *If God would choose to work through radiation, what is that to me that I should be filled with such anxiety and dread?* I thought.

My next appointment was with Dr. Petersen, radiation oncologist. I liked her immediately. She exuded kindness and gentleness, and I felt at ease with her professionalism.

"First, we calculate the exact location of where the radiation beams intersect and then we will mark you permanently, like a dot tattoo, so each time you come for treatment, it will be precise," she explained.

Even though she patiently answered my questions, I did not want to commit, but I had no other choice, so March 1, 2007 was set for my first radiation treatment.

"Lord, when I look at what lies before me, I can become completely overwhelmed. Help me to be concerned for only the day at hand. I know that when we get to eternity, it will always be the day at hand. We need not worry nor be concerned for tomorrow for that day never comes; only the day at hand. Please help me deal with today," I prayed.

First, I was 'tattooed' with three small dots – one on each side and one in the middle of my abdomen where the radiation beams would cross precisely on target.

Each radiation treatment consisted of nine beams of light with each beam lasting between five to eight seconds. As I lay on an elevated bed, a machine hovered over me. With each beam, the arm of the machine would rotate a little until it completed its circular path around me.

By the fifth beam of light, I felt extremely hot inside—like my blood was boiling within me. After the eighth beam, one of the x-ray technologists entered the room and made an adjustment on the underside of the bed.

"I feel extremely hot," I said, without moving a muscle.

"Really? That's strange. Well, it can't be from the radiation," he assured me, as he left the room.

I wasn't so sure, however. The very uncomfortable hot feeling lasted for another twenty minutes after treatment was completed.

"I feel like I'm boiling inside," I told Burt. "I don't know if I can do this."

He held me tight to his chest. "I've been praying that if there is some other way…"

Just like Jesus prayed in the Garden of Gethsemane, I thought. *But there was no other way for Him, nor was there for me.*

The second treatment the following day also brought a hot feeling, but not nearly as severe. The only other side effect I felt was pain in my left leg which was attributed to possible nerve irritation from the radiation, and that "it should settle down."

On my fourth day of radiation as Burt and I sat in the radiology waiting area, I thought of my three previous cancer surgeries with their fears and trepidations. No matter what level of trust to which the Lord brought me, His peace and strength consistently dissipated those fears and trepidations. I am called to a deeper faith when I cannot sense God near me. It seemed that at just the right time, He supplied all I needed—my faith grew—not without struggle and stretching, but always with purpose.

Sometimes God would surprise me with words of encouragement like the older male volunteer who offered snacks or beverages to those seated in the radiation department waiting area.

This man approached us and after offering us a cookie or juice, he stood directly in front of me and said, "Sixteen years ago, I was sitting here. When I was told I would be permanently disabled from the radiation, I was angry and after four days, I finally settled down and that's when I heard a still small voice say, 'My grace is sufficient for you.' I thought you might want to hear that."

"Yes, I am glad to hear that. I hope you are doing well and thank you for encouraging me," I said puzzled as to why he would speak to me in such a way. That glimpse into another person's soul uplifted me, but at the same time, I wondered what his words directed exclusively to me could mean.

Burt and I drove the eighty-five miles to Rochester every day for my radiation treatments. After one week of driving our daily commute, I mumbled, "This seems like a lot of wasted time. Don't you think?"

"Not at all. I get to spend every morning with my bride," Burt answered with a smile. "What could be better?"

His smile was sincere. "You're right. I need to change my attitude. I'll try to look at this as a great opportunity to be together. I'm sorry for complaining."

He smiled tenderly.

My Martha personality changed from grumbling about not being able to accomplish anything during the time spent in the car to one of delight at being able to spend quality time with my husband.

From then on, I packed a 'car-nic' lunch to eat on the way home and chided myself to remain optimistic rather than be a complainer.

Towards the end of the five weeks of radiation, I met with several surgeons who would be involved in my surgery: vascular, orthopedic, urology, in addition to the colorectal surgeon. Each surgeon, in turn, forewarned me of the possible complications of the surgery: blood clots, damaged veins, loss of muscle control in my left leg, damage to my ureter tube that may require a bag for urine output—temporary or long-term, and that my cancer may not respond which meant that I would be at the end of my options.

I swallowed hard. I sighed and nodded ever so slightly.

Surgery was set for April 25, 2007.

"Lord, as I look to You, help me to know You are looking at me," I pleaded quietly.

The day before surgery, my sister, Gayle flew in from New York. I was glad to have her with me. Our three daughters and their families arrived at Methodist Hospital in Rochester the morning of surgery. Prayer warriors from church, nearby, and across the nation were in prayer. I sensed the presence of Jesus as I went into surgery.

With Gayle's permission, I will insert her journaling of my surgery exactly as she wrote it.

4-25-07   Day of surgery (*Italics* are mine)

5:45am   Surgery day. Burt & Rita, Brian (*son-in-law*), LaDawn (*daughter*), Ryan (*grandson*), and Gayle (*sister*) to Methodist Hospital in Rochester for admission. Chaplain Scott came by to see Rita, prayed with family for Rita's protection and for God's wisdom to flow through the hands of the surgeons. We were to be apprised of her status every 2 hours.

6:50am Rita tearfully hugged each family member, with each whispering their own tendered-hearted message to her. Then it was time for her to go to pre-op.

Surgery was scheduled to begin at 8:15. In that first hour, a stint was inserted and a cystogram done. She was then moved to a new, larger OR – her 4 teams ready. Prep took another hour and by 9:30am, she began her journey with God and the surgeons He had assembled.

10:30am Our first update. Rita doing well; that was encouraging. Surgery would be complicated because of location of tumor. That was troublesome.

11:00am   Pastor Dan arrived. That was comforting and reassuring. After initial greetings, we gathered in the prayer room again. The prayer time throughout the day kept hearts focused on God's grace and our eyes on the cross of Jesus.

12:30pm Second update. Surgery progressing slowly; lots of bleeding, tumor deep. It appears kidney ok and no need for colostomy. Day beginning to get long for those of us waiting but filled time with talk, prayer, and Scrabble.

2:30pm Six hours into surgery. Third update. Surgeon still working to get at tumor. This would be our last update as RN going off duty. She would make arrangements for crucial info to be relayed to our family.

4:00pm Seven and a half hours after the start of surgery. We were called to surgery consultation area for meeting with Dr. Dozois. He said surgery was complicated and difficult – Rita lost 6 units of blood, received transfusions, and fluid to add volume to blood. 95% of tumor removed – but not a clean margin. Cells attached to nerve endings against pelvic bone. Too dangerous to try to remove these cells. Then he said it, "The cancer would come back." As he spoke to us, Rita was receiving intra-operative radiation followed by replacement of stint. He expected she would be in surgery another couple of hours yet. When he left, we prayed again through tear-filled eyes, and then returned to the 10th floor oncology waiting room.

7:30pm Rita's surgery was over – 11 hours after it began. She was on her way to recovery where she would remain for 1-2 hours before being moved to ICU. We all made update phone calls, thankful her surgery was over, and yet, apprehensive about what lay ahead for her.

8:45pm She was brought to ICU – edemas and ashen. Her body had been traumatized, that was evident, but she seemed to be resting comfortably. It would take some time to get her hooked up to the monitors, etc. but finally Burt, accompanied by LaDawn and Ryan, was able to see his beloved wife once again. Tubes and all, she was probably as beautiful to him at this time as she was the day she walked down the aisle to her handsome groom. Shelly, René, and Gayle were the next ones to see her.

10:40pm   RN could not get a pulse in her lower left leg. She called for Dr. Bard to evaluate. Dr. Bard observed weakness in her left side and was also unable to pick up a pulse. He called for Dr. Bologna (attending). He, too, did an exam and called in Dr. Houghton. Concern increased and he called Dr. Dozois. Albumin was started and pushed rapidly. Platelets were started…and the vascular surgeon was called in. Still much uncertainty but the possibility for more surgery was being discussed. Rita's body temp was still low but that now seemed to be the least of the concerns. Time was around 11:30pm.

Dr. Dozois had said if sutures in the vein popped, Rita would need surgery immediately—an indication of this would be a drop in BP and an increase in heart rate. Vascular surgeon in consult with another vascular surgeon; agreed she needed a CT scan with contrast to determine what was going on. IF…too many ifs. If it was a blood clot compressing the artery, Rita would need immediate surgery. IF the veins were involved, surgery might be urgent, but not an emergency. IF Rita responded to current interventions, surgery could be avoided. They had to start with the CT scan.

4-26-07 One day after surgery.

2:20am   Rita taken down to CT scan w/contrast. Results will determine what interventions, if any, would be necessary.

2:55am   Rita came back from the CT scan. Waiting for radiologist to read scan.

3:30am Dr. Bard informed René and Gayle that the CT scan showed a clot in the artery – doctors to confer over next hour to hour and a half – vascular team and Dozois' team to decide next course of action. Decision should be made around 5:00am. IF surgery is the option, Dr. Bard thought the time frame would be somewhere between 6:00-9:00am.

5:15am Burt received call from Methodist ICU (Dr. Houghten) seeking Burt's authorization for emergency surgery for a blood clot to be done at St. Mary's Hospital. Rita transported to St. Mary's via ambulance and believed to have been in surgery around 6:00am.

10:00am Vascular surgeon called Burt and indicated she'd be out of surgery soon.

11:00am Rita out of surgery (5 hours to remove clot). From recovery, she was moved to ICU at St. Mary's. She was pretty well sedated. Dozois spoke to Burt indicating that, from his perspective, Rita was holding steady.

Throughout afternoon, Rita received platelets and other blood products to help stop the oozing from surgical sights, needle pricks, etc. as blood too thin. Doctors working that fine line between too thick and too thin blood volume. If use of blood fluids doesn't result in cessation of bleeding, other interventions may become necessary, including possible surgery.

Update calls continue to be made and prayers across the country continue to be offered up on Rita's behalf. Burt's heart is heavy– his deep love for Rita and his overwhelming sense of helplessness are evident. We talk of that elusive and iffy day when he's blessed to be taking his beautiful bride home.

Dr.Bersoun, vascular surgeon, was called in for a consult. He completed exam and met with critical care doctors to determine treatment options for clotting issues.

6:00pm Shelly & Scott (*daughter and son-in-law*), René (*daughter*), and Gayle (*sister*) out for quick supper – and more update calls. Burt took a break, returned to the hotel for a little uninterrupted sleep. LaDawn and Mike, Ryan and Faith stayed with Rita. During this time, the critical care doctor turned off the ventilator. Lungs heavy with fluid and breathing without ventilator was difficult. The ventilator turned on immediately – breathing much easier.

8:00pm Shelly and Scott and René stayed with Rita; LaDawn, Mike and the kids headed back to the hotel. One nurse assigned only to Rita; to sit bedside all night. Rita resting comfortably. Burt and René stayed at the hospital overnight.

4-27-07 Two days after surgery.

Burt and René came back to the hotel about 7:00am, showered, and brought us up to date. Although Rita had a 'comfortable' night, she received 2 units of blood plus other fluids. So far, she has received 30 liters of ICV fluid. She's still a little puffy. Hemoglobin is 7.

All returned to hospital between 7:30-9:00am. RN stated Rita's belly was a bit distended and urine output was diminished. Reasons unknown, but could possibly be some internal bleeding and possibly decreased kidney functioning. Labs were done and RN was waiting for results. In the meantime, RN explained a renal ultrasound was ordered. Lab results back – Hemoglobin is up to 9.6, and kidney levels (BUN, creatinine) within normal limits. Very encouraging results.

10:00am Renal ultrasound done to determine if any problems with kidney or any compressions.

11:00am Critical care team came in to review their care plans for next 24-48 hours. Rita to remain on the ventilator, but she is breathing over the ventilator (vent set at 12 reps. she's breathing at a slightly higher rate). She is on Protonix as a precaution against GI distress. She has boot on left foot as it was slightly cooler than right foot. She will continue to receive fluids, but CCT believes they will be able to discontinue w/in 24-48 hours. CCT is comfortable with her status – given she's had 2 major surgeries within 24 hours. Hearing this was certainly reassuring and encouraging.

Rita seems to be stabilizing and looking like she was out of this rough time. Burt and Gayle decided to head for home. René (*daughter*), LaDawn and Mike (*daughter and husband*), Ryan and Faith (*grandchildren*) stayed with Rita.

René made the update calls to immediate family – keeping us informed of Rita's status. Around 8:30 p.m., René called Gayle and said that Rita's belly was distended, and incisions were being stretched and were starting to open. Doctors not alarmed by this, and steri-striped her incisions. Rita was given two sponge baths, back massage and was repositioned. She seemed to be resting comfortably.

Sometime around 10:30 pm, Rita was given Lasix to take off some of the fluid. René found a quiet room and grabbed some much-needed sleep.

4-28-07 Three days after surgery.

2:30am René checked on Rita – still resting comfortably.

6:30am René is back with Rita and provided updates throughout the day.

8:30am Burt returned to Rochester eager to see his beautiful wife.

LaDawn and Mike, Ryan, and Faith stayed in a motel Friday night and were back Sat. morning for that precious time with Rita, before they headed back home.

Gayle had planned to visit Mom on Sat. (saw her on Friday) wanting desperately for Mom to understand that Rita was in the hospital following her surgery. Mom was too confused by Alzheimer's to grasp.

In one of René's updates, Rita had been given another dose of Lasix – she put out 100 cc's of urine, but BP dropped to a dangerous level. Rita's sedative decreased somewhat resulting in some agitation. Ironically, they had to give her more fluid so BP would stabilize.

4:00pm René's called to say she and Burt probably would be staying; this driven more by RN than complications with Rita.

6:45pm Evening of the third day after surgery.

René called Gayle. "Mom is not doing well." BP dropping again (74/43), and possible internal bleeding. Vascular team notified; emergency labs drawn (Hbg. down to 7).

Another unit of blood given, then it was wait and see. Doctors said her body was giving them mixed signals; labs coming back normal but, heart rate up and BP would not stay elevated. Drainage from the surgery site overflowed the container, so doctors wanted to try more cautious approaches first. They discussed doing another CT scan but wanted her to stabilize first before risking moving her to the CT area. Pastor Dan updated.

9:00pm Doctors continue to monitor Rita. She tried to tell us something she was feeling, but could not speak because of the ventilator. Pushed in another 500 cc's of fluid; did emergency labs and ordered medication to bring BP up. Earlier, Rita had been given Ativan in IV to deepen her sedation as she had awakened a bit and experienced significant panic. More Ativan every 6 hours as needed.

4-29-07 Four days after surgery.

12:30am Rita resting comfortably. BP stabilizing.

1:00am Long discussion w/vascular surgeon who explained the effects of pushed fluid and how blood vessels react. The vascular team is still in 'wait and see' mode, but if Rita's BP remains elevated and drainage tube continues to run clear, further surgery becoming more remote.

Rita had a nice back rub and was repositioned. (This was uncomfortable for her.) She was suctioned – became slightly agitated, but relaxed as soon as suctioning was completed. Anticipated she'll have chest x-ray around 2:00am; standard procedure for any patient who has been intubated.

7:00am Rita comfortable throughout night. BP came back up, heart rate dropped back to normal, and urine output remained at about 30 cc's per hour. Burt, René, and Gayle stayed with her throughout the morning.

11:00am Vascular team came in. They were pleased that her vitals had remained stable; that the drainage from surgical site appeared to be clearing. They were still concerned about the fluid in her body. She needs to expel this fluid before it is safe to take her off the ventilator. She required suctioning several times – does not like this. Rita is unable to talk but does well communicating with facial expressions and hand gestures. And she has not lost her sense of humor. René told Rita we know how much she misses Tigger (*family dog*), so a picture of Tigger was next to her bed. Rita mustered up a small laugh!

A little while later, Rita tried to tell us something she was feeling, but could not speak because of the ventilator. René grabbed a piece of paper and pen and gave them to Rita. She wrote one word. But she wrote each letter on top of the other letters, so it was hard to decipher what she said. René studied it and finally figured it out. Rita wrote the word *numb*. Didn't know what she meant.

Brian *(son-in-law),* Michael and Jesse (grandsons) came down around 11:30am. Michael told Rita all about his track meet while Brian tenderly wiped her brow with a cool, damp cloth. What a precious moment.

Earlier in the day, Rita able to let us know she wanted us to hold her hand and talk to her. At one point in the morning, she opened her eyes making direct eye contact with Gayle. Her eyes looked so beautiful!

80

Her nurse asked to do one-on-one with Rita, and doted on her.

3:30pm Nurse gave Rita a bath, changed her dressings, gave her a back rub, and repositioned her.

4:30pm We all came back into the room and prayed.

5:30pm René, Brian and boys, and Gayle headed home. Burt stayed with Rita until ventilator is removed. According to CCU (*critical care unit*) charge nurse, not likely to happen until Friday,

5-4-07 Nine days after surgery.

Concern is for Rita's comfort and safety.
Rita continued to recover for the next five days.

5-9-07 Fourteen days after surgery.

Finally, Rita came home from hospital. She did some writing and shared these thoughts: *'I've aged beyond my mother'* and *'Everything has changed. Two weeks ago, I was home, feeling great. I had surgery and have complications that are permanent. It doesn't seem real. I need time to absorb this.'*

As her new reality began to set in, so did a new awareness such as developing new routines. Rita shared this thought: *'Missing communing with the Lord during my morning walks' and the structure of my life before surgery.*

5-15-07 Twenty days after surgery

Today was a long day for Rita – she had visitors, many phone calls, did a little exercising, and had no nap. She is tired and her discouragement is evident. "I feel like I can't get over the hump to feeling good again." Though discouraged, she is determined; this afternoon, she planted flowers in the front flower planter. Reminded me of the verse that says, 'Blessed is the man who perseveres under trial; for once he has stood the test, he will receive the crown of life, which the Lord has promised to those who love Him.'

5-18-07 Twenty three days after surgery

Rita did not go to church today saying, "I'm not ready for that yet." She saw Mom today. Mom in her own far-away place was unable to respond much to Rita. Rita said, "I am saddened that Mom had no reaction."

It is Mother's Day and René hosted a celebratory dinner. It was a good visit and lots of good, heartfelt talk. At the end of the day, Rita said, "Every hour that goes by, I am recognizing more and more that I am blessed to be nested in Christian support."

Chapter 10

Recovery

As I read Gayle's journaling, I can honestly say, "I am glad I was not aware of those many days in the hospital." Truly, I was in the valley of the shadow of death. I am so grateful for those who have brought me before the Lord in prayer, without ceasing, when I could not pray.

As I stood at the edge of the valley of the shadow of death, the sun shone down, and I was able to look back in my mind's eye and see one set of footprints. I knew it was then that the Lord carried me. How true are the words: "Shadows are made because there is a bright light somewhere." I thought of our pastor's words, "The grace that orders our pain is the same grace that sustains us in the darkness."

My first realization of one of the possible complications of which the doctors had forewarned me about came while I was still recovering in the hospital. My left foot was completely numb except for icy tingles each time someone touched my toes. I had large areas of numbness in my leg and no muscle strength. I was told that between the radiation and the surgery, the main nerve in my leg had been permanently damaged. My ability to walk was compromised.

Most of the time surrounding the hospital recovery blurred into time, but I did remember a couple of incidents. One happened on a warm, sunny day. Burt took me in a wheelchair to the small park on the hospital campus. He braked my wheelchair and sat on a park bench and together we soaked up the warm sunshine.

After a short time, a man walking his dog happened by. We chatted about his dog and then I asked, "What brings you to Rochester?"

"I am here for testing and as yet, they don't know what's wrong." He glanced at his dog and suddenly tried to choke back tears. "I have to get going," he said. Then he did an unusual thing. He bent down and gave me a hug.

I sensed his hug was his desperate need to connect, so I asked, "Do you want us to pray for you?"

"Yes," he said through unrestrained tears and sat down next to Burt. We joined hands and prayed for his medical needs.

"Do you know Jesus?" I asked.

"I have my own ideas," he answered.

Burt and I told him that because God is holy and man is sinful, there can be no relationship between a holy God and sinful man, but because of God's great love for mankind, He sent His only Son, Jesus, to come to earth in the flesh to die on the cross for the sins of the world, and whoever believed in Him, his sins would be forgiven, and he could be assured of going to heaven for eternity.

We talked for several minutes together before he stood up, still weeping. He gave me another hug and shook Burt's hand.

"Before you go, could I ask you; what made you stop to talk to us?" I asked.

"You seemed like nice people."

Was it because I was in a wheelchair? And if I had not been in a wheelchair, would we not have had this opportunity to talk to this stranger? That was my first realization that God can use me to reach out to others regardless of my physical ineptness.

Another memorable time was when the doctors made their usual daily rounds. One of the rotating doctors stopped back alone after rounds to talk with Burt and me. He wanted to talk to us about the Lord and was delighted to learn that we were already believers. He made it a point to come back every day simply to talk about the Lord.

Chapter 11

Sufficient Grace

After I had been home from the hospital a couple of weeks still reeling from the words that my inability to walk normally was permanent, and that I would always need either a walker or a cane, I sat in my chair by the window reading. I read 2 Corinthians 12:8-9 where Paul says: "Concerning this thorn in the flesh, I entreated the Lord three times that it might depart from me. And He has said to me, 'My grace is sufficient for you, for power is perfected in weakness.'" Familiar words that I had read several times in the Bible suddenly grabbed my attention in a fresh way.

"What does that mean?" I asked the Lord. 'My grace is sufficient for you.' I remembered the elderly male volunteer from the radiation department three months earlier, and how he had said those exact words to me when I was perfectly able to walk. At that time, I wondered what significance his words had for me.

And now, I came upon those same words again. "My grace is sufficient for you." *Very perplexing*.

Another couple of weeks passed. Once again, I sat in my favorite chair by the window that overlooks our backyard. It was through much prayer and contemplation of my inability to walk without the aid of a cane or walker that I gradually came to accept what must be. The words "My grace is sufficient for you" nudged my mind like an encore. Ahh, I thought. That's what those words mean! Not without a significant struggle, but nevertheless, I realized that when I accepted what must be, I grasped the depth of the Lord's words that truly His grace is sufficient for me.

I had to allow my circumstances, my thorn in the flesh, to do the job of provoking humility in me that I might see God's greatness and change my perspective away from me to Him.

As I look back and see the road signs marking a positive change in my journey on earth, they all appeared in places of difficulty. As Beth Moore said, "Every person who seems liberated to love, to feel compassion, and to rejoice has been on the battlefield," and "If we're not walking with God when trials come, we miss the full measure of strength He has for us along the way."

Although it is human nature to want to avoid pain at all costs, we can learn from painful experiences. As the psalmist said in Psalm 119:7, "It is good for me that I have been afflicted that I may learn your statutes." I give personal testimony to the truth of those words found in Scripture.

It took me several weeks before I accepted what must be in order to know God's grace. I cannot imagine how long some people must deal with suffering or sickness or disability for themselves or for a loved one, especially if that loved one is a child, before they can accept the grace of God—that His strength is made perfect in our weakness. God will heal every suffering one way or the other in due time. Of that we can be certain.

Revelation 21:4 says, "He will wipe away every tear from their eyes, and death shall be no more, neither shall there be mourning nor crying nor pain anymore, for the former things have passed away." (ESV) It is this same God who gives grace and compassion to those who suffer. It is for His purpose.

I have come to know His peace in the calm and in the storms, but *only* when I yield to God with complete acceptance of His total grace in *any* given circumstance.

May I encourage you to remember: wherever there are dark shadows, there is a bright light on the other side. Do you see God's immense love for each of us? Be reassured that He is with you in season and out of season whether it is in times of calmness or times of storm.

So, my friend, no matter how fierce the battle or how lonely the journey, whether in the valley of the shadow of death or the mountaintop of sunshine, there is One who will strengthen you and will never leave you nor forsake you. His name is Jesus.

Chapter 12

A Reminder

I was told by the surgeon that the more abdominal surgeries a person has, the more likely they are to have obstruction. "Each surgery increases the chances for obstruction twenty percent.

And I had three abdominal surgeries.

In April, 2008, one year after my last surgery and radiation, I had extreme stomach pain. Burt took me to ER at a local hospital. After x-rays, a CT scan, and an MRI it was determined I did indeed have an obstruction. A NG tube was inserted through my nose, taped in place, and fed down my throat into my stomach.

The pain became tolerable the more my stomach was decompressed. I hated the feel of the tube against the back of my throat, but I accepted it as it was the only means to alleviate my pain. I had an IV to keep my electrolytes in balance and to counter dehydration.

What would it be like if I could not eat again—even if for only a month? As I lay in the hospital bed, my thoughts drifted to the Biblical account of Jesus and how He had nothing to eat for forty days. During that time, Satan tempted Him to turn the stones into bread. Jesus had nothing to eat for forty days – I was one day, and I had an IV!

Jesus said to Satan, "Man shall not live by bread alone, but by every word that proceeds from the mouth of God."

In that one statement, I believe Jesus laid out a principle that we all need to understand—we cannot maintain physical life at the neglect of our spiritual life. We must feed on the Word of God as well. "Give us this day our daily bread," are words found in the Lord's Prayer—food to nourish our bodies and spiritual substance to nurture our souls.

After three days in the hospital, I was transferred via ambulance to St. Mary's Hospital in Rochester. I had more x-rays and a CT scan. The doctors said, "We want to treat this conservatively in hopes of avoiding another surgery. We'll wait a couple of weeks to see if it will resolve on its own."

I looked incredulously at the physician. "A couple of weeks?"

"Ninety percent chance it will resolve. Walking helps." He sounded confident.

"I'm going to have to change my address, you know."

He smiled as he left the room.

A PICC line was inserted in the inside of my upper right arm through which I was given nutrients and lipids. I was in for the long haul.

"Heavenly Father, help me through this."

A little while later, a nurse asked Burt where he was staying.

"I'm staying at the Town & Country," he answered.

She looked puzzled. "Is that a new motel?"

"No, it's on the 4th level of the parking ramp."

She looked at him with question marks all over her face.

"It's the van I drive."

We all had to laugh.

How good it is to see humor, I thought.

Burt and I started our multiple, daily walks in the halls of St. Mary's Hospital. Ten days after the onset of my obstruction, I was given a very small bowl of creamy chicken soup. Almost instantly, I had stomach pain and threw up. The NG tube was re-inserted, suction began, and IVs were re-started.

Almost two weeks passed since the onset of the obstruction when the surgeon stopped by to let me know they were going to give me a few more days, and then possible surgery.

Three days later, I was allowed small sips of water – no more than two tablespoons per hour. *Seriously?* The cool water tasted wonderfully refreshing, but I was careful to sip only a tiny swallow at a time.

April 27, twenty days from the onset, I was given a small amount of clear liquids. By the next day, I had stomach pain, and my blood pressure and heart rate were up, and I was feeling nauseated. A NG tube was re-inserted.
The next morning, the team of doctors came into my room. "We cannot let you go on any longer or your bowels will never wake up," the lead doctor said. I was transferred to Methodist Hospital for surgery the following day.

During surgery, Dr. Dozois cut a band of adhesions around the small intestine and corrected two other possible problem areas. "The good news? No cancer!" he said.

It was one of the less complicated surgeries I've had and recovery took only three days.

At first, I was given small amounts of clear liquid which I tolerated well, so I was increased to full liquids and then to little amounts of soft food. What a delight to be able to eat food again!

During this period, Burt and I spent much time reading the Bible. We read how Jesus healed a leper, the blind man, a daughter of an official, and even raised a man from the dead. "There's nothing, nothing too difficult for the Lord," Burt said.

I nodded in agreement

Burt read 1 Thessalonians 5:17, "…in everything give thanks for this is God's will for you." It's true. Even in adversity, one can always find blessings for which to be thankful. I discovered that grumbling leads to bitterness, but gratitude leads to contentment.

On May 8, 2008, I was discharged from the hospital— one month after being admitted.

Excerpt

I decided to add an excerpt of a letter from a mother of young children who was deep in the struggles of cancer. I loved her wanting to press forward for the benefit of her children, and of others who are stricken with cancer. Her name was Kara.

She wrote, "There is life to live today, join me. There are hurting hearts that need to hear of the goodness of Jesus—even when life is hard. Let's go tell that story. We have children heading into school, life, growth— they need our prayers today. We have a lot asked of us with each breath—let's press deeply into Jesus and find the best of life. There's so much that wants to steal our joy, rob us of today—for me, it's cancer. What is it for you? These unwelcomed guests—well, they exist and pretending they don't is simply a lie. How do we meet the hard in our story, live it honestly, then head out into life and live?"

My Personal Note to You

I am writing this personal note to you, beloved friend. You may be suffering the anguish of cancer or some other dreaded disease, or someone you love may be the one suffering, I understand your anxieties and your heartache. And it is with much empathy that I offer to pray. Please join me.

"Heavenly Father, You are LORD of the heavens and the earth. Your holiness is unsurpassed. Your grace is abundant beyond measure. Your unconditional love is never-ending. Your mercy is new every morning, and Your promises are completely trustworthy. Your word proves true for You are a shield to all who take refuge in You."

"Help us to pray earnestly for all who are in affliction, for those under trial, for those in persecution, and for those in adverse situations, that each one may know Your presence with them, that each one will remain faithful, and that Your peace that surpasses all understanding will guard and keep their hearts and minds in Christ Jesus. Give each one strength to persevere. Grant healing from cancer and the effects of its treatment according to Your good and perfect will."

"Help us to realize that when we patiently endure, it becomes evidence of our salvation in You, Christ Jesus."

"Instill in us the truth that untested faith is not faith at all, but faith is that which has stood the test that we may receive the crown of life which You promised to all who believe; to those who love You."

"Thank You, Father, for I ask these things in Jesus' name."

Rita Kroon

"For I know the plans that I have for you," declares the Lord, "plans for welfare and not for calamity to give you a future and a hope." Jeremiah 29:11

Epilogue

Small wooden cross

A few weeks after I received the small, wooden cross from the impeccably dressed man in the hallway, a friend of mine was going to have knee replacement surgery. Regina was terrified of the anesthesia because of previous complications. Burt and I went to the hospital to be with her the morning of her surgery.

I gave her the wooden cross and explained how I had received it. "Would you like to have it?" I asked. Regina gladly accepted it and after a brief prayer, she proceeded into surgery.

She later reiterated that when her surgeon saw the cross, he asked the entire surgical team to take a moment and pray together for my friend. Surgery was successful and Regina had only minimal effects from the anesthesia.

****

My brother, Rob

Rob was two years older than me, and as kids, I would tag behind him wherever he went. As teens, we hung out with the same friends and teased each other who had the best car. As adults, we both raised our families spending every holiday together.

****

Geri, from Florida, is a leiomyosarcoma survivor who called to advise me to get a second opinion at Mayo Clinic in Rochester. Her brother and my brother worked together.

****

Sharon and Rita

Sharon and I started out as next-door neighbors, then friends, then sisters in Christ, and finally comrades in cancer. Sharon was

100

diagnosed with stage 4 lung cancer two years after my last cancer surgery. We spent many hours on the phone talking, crying, and encouraging one another. We both re-read Max Lucado's book <u>It's Not about Me</u>.

When she lay in bed at her home with death crouching at her bedside, I asked her if she would like me to play some of her favorite Christian music.

"No," she said softly, "I'd rather listen to the voice of God than the songs of men."

Sharon died shortly thereafter.

****

Our granddaughter Rachel

We traveled to Iowa to celebrate Rachel's fourth birthday. After cake 'n' ice cream, she asked if I wanted to play 'princess' with her.

"I'd love to play," I answered.

"Okay, I'll be the princess and you be the queen."
"All right," I agreed waiting for her

instructions as to how we would play 'princess' this time.

She looked at my cane and thought for a minute. She said, "I'll be the princess and you be the queen with the magic walking wand!" She was delighted to have a grandma with a magic walking wand, and I felt special too. How could I not with a title like that!

****

Four in a million

While at a car show in 2009, my friend Deb said, "I have a friend in North Dakota that has the same type of cancer you have." Deb put us in touch with one another and Judy and I became instant friends.

"Do you realize how special we are?" Judy asked. "We are four in a million!"

"Yes, and now I know all four of us," I said.

A year later, Judy stepped off the battlefield and stepped into eternity with her Savior.

Our youngest daughter

Shelly and Scott now
have seven children.

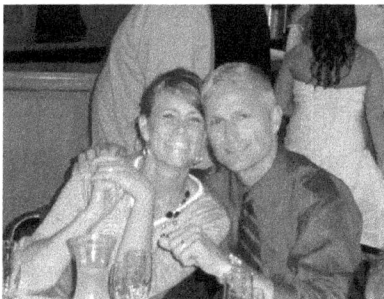

****

Our second daughter

René and Brian
have five children.

****

Our oldest daughter

LaDawn and Mike with two of their five children, Ryan and Faith.

****

My sister, Gayle

Gayle moved from New York and continues to live in Minnesota.

****

My Mother

My mother died at the age of 92. I was able to be with her the last hour of her life on earth before entering the presence of the Lord. I put my cheek next to her cheek and spoke into her good ear. "Mom, Rita is here, and so is Jesus." Then I recited the twenty-third psalm to her and kissed her on her cheek. She relaxed as a peace seemed to settle over her. A few minutes later she was gone.

****

Our cabin

We sold our cabin in 2010. "Retired people should not have to work so hard," Burt said.

****

Our Daughter, René

Seven years after I "graduated" from regular check-ups for my cancer, we received the devastating news that our daughter, René (46) was diagnosed with stage 3-C ovarian cancer. The news sucked the air right out of me. It was worse than when I heard those dreaded words spoken to me, "You have cancer." Rene´ underwent surgery at St. Mary's Hospital in Rochester followed by eighteen rounds of chemo. Although René is on chemo pills that target her cancer, the cancer has returned. She is under care once again at Mayo Clinic in Rochester. Her cancer is in its early stages, so she has not begun treatment yet. She is still feeling great, but the road ahead is obscured in the unknown. We are praying for healing according to His will and His grace for René and family if God has others plans for her.

****

It is with a sad and grieving heart that I write this final chapter in René's life:

On Tuesday, January 19, 2021, at 6:20 pm, René (Kroon) Maleski laid down her sword. She fought the good fight, she has finished the race, she has kept the faith. Henceforth there is laid up for René the crown of righteousness, which the Lord, the righteous judge, will award her on that Day, and not only to René, but to all who have loved His appearing. By the time you read this, René will have heard the words, "Well done thou good and faithful servant. Enter into the joy of your Lord."

René accomplished what she was called to do – share the gospel of Jesus Christ with others, and that she did. Her eternal future is sure, and her hope is now a reality.

****

My husband, Burt

After a whirlwind courtship of five months, I married the love of my life - Burt Kroon. Burt was an awesome husband and a godly man. We did life together – everything from raising our three daughters to owning motorcycles and classic cars. We shared faith in our Lord Jesus Christ. Three months after we celebrated our 56th anniversary, we contracted covid 19 – together. Burt was hospitalized, but because of hospital protocol, I was not allowed to be with him except for one visit during his 13-day hospitalization. He passed away – alone. I pleaded with the Lord all that first night asking over and over, "Why, Lord, was I not allowed to be with Burt?" In the morning, I resolved to let it go. I was not going to get an answer. But I asked one last time, "Why, Lord, was I not allowed to be with Burt?" He answered, "Because I was." With those three words I felt the peace of God that surpasses all understanding that keeps my heart and mind in Christ Jesus.

****

Psalm 23

"The Lord is my Shepherd; I shall not be in want. He makes me to lie down in green pastures; He leads me beside the still waters. He restores my soul; He leads me in the paths of righteousness for His name's sake. Even though I walk through the valley of the shadow of death, I will fear no evil; for You are with me; Your rod (protection) and Your staff (guidance), they comfort me. You prepare a table before me in the presence of my enemies. You anoint my head with oil; my cup runs over. Surely goodness and mercy shall follow me all the days of my life; and I will dwell in the house of the Lord forever."

Meet the Author

Rita Kroon was born in Minneapolis, but raised in St. Paul, MN. She graduated from Sibley High School and received her AA degree in speech/communications from Lakewood Community College.

She is an author, blogger, and Bible study leader. She has written novels (Contemporary and historical), Bible studies, devotionals, wildlife magazine articles, children's short stories, poetry, and a humorous newspaper column "Rita Raps it up."

She is a 16-year cancer survivor.

Rita lives in Lexington, MN,

Other Books by Rita Kroon

Womanhood: Becoming a Woman of Virtue is an eight-week, interactive Bible study of eight inspirational women of the Old Testament and is suitable for individual or group setting. There are two sections: in-depth for the woman who likes to linger in the Word or condensed for the woman on the go. Explore the lives of Eve, Sarah, Rebekah, Rachel, Miriam, Deborah, Tamar, and Esther–ordinary women who find themselves in unprecedented circumstances. Be inspired by their faith, encouraged through their hardships, and challenged by their choices and decisions as you seek to become a woman of virtue.

ISBN: 9780989198554

40 Days of Assurance is a daily devotional intended to give you assurance in your walk with God, or with your parenting skills, or with relationships, or with a lack of confidence with who you are as a person. Sometimes we just need loving arms around us; to be assured that everything will work out. Bring your empty cup to the Lord that he may fill it with your daily portion of His grace, and discover the peace of God that surpasses all understanding that will keep your heart and mind in Christ Jesus.

ISBN: 9780989198530

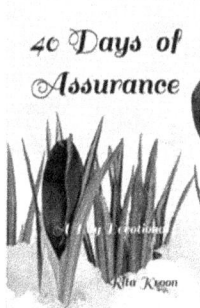

40 Days of Encouragement is a daily devotional when you may feel like giving up, or you are bombarded with negative thoughts, or you have lost all hope, or you are despairing over broken relationships, or when you see the future through the bleakness of the past. Be encouraged. God is a reservoir of strength. He plans to give you a future and a hope. Come, drink deeply of God's word and be encouraged.

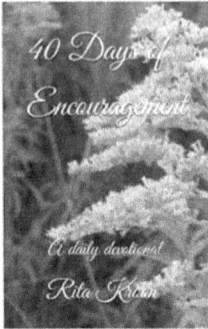

ISBN: **9780989198547**

40 Days in the Wilderness is a daily devotional that gives insight to strengthen and to nourish you as you journey through your wilderness – a drought in your spiritual walk? A desert in your marriage with no oasis in sight? A dry spell at work or at school? Lacking peace amidst the chaos? Whatever your wilderness, take heart. Bring your empty cup to the Lord that He may fill it with your daily portion of His grace. Find the faith needed to sustain you and be nourished and refreshed.

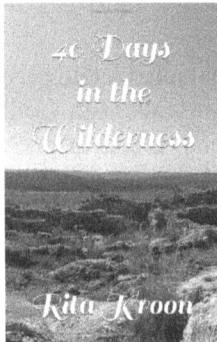

ISBN: 9780989198509

Kiss Your Mommy Goodbye is a Christian novel. In his desperate quest to provide love and stability as a part-time father to young Maddy, Mike does the unthinkable. His actions net far more disastrous results than he could have ever imagined, and the very one he tried to protect would suffer the repercussions of his decision. In this riveting tale, a young, divorced man struggles to reconcile and rebuild broken relationships and to find peace with God and with others. **ISBN: 9780989198561**

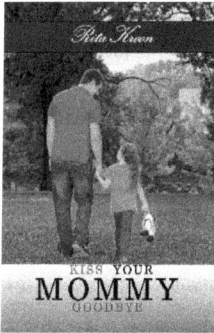

Praying the Scriptures is a collection of prayers and promises taken from God's Word, since no word of God shall be void of power. When words cannot be found to say what is on your heart, this collection of prayers is meant to guide you during those times of solitude. If praying is unfamiliar to you, or perhaps has long ago been abandoned, this book provides one way to begin afresh. There is no prayer like that which forms itself in the words and thoughts of Scripture, for there are no other words on earth spoken by man that have neither more power nor more truth than God's Word.

Respond to the Lord's invitation to enter into a more intimate relationship with Him by praying His word.

ISBN: 9780989198585

Letters from the Past is historical fiction. Seven women of the Bible write personal letters to today's woman. Each woman reveals the emotional impact that infertility, rape, incest, deception and betrayal, and family dysfunction had on her. In each of their stories, trial turns to triumph when the thread of God's faithfulness is traced through these women of ancient times to the women of the twenty first century. Today's woman will be challenged and encouraged, will find hope for the oppressed, and will celebrate the accomplishments of Sarah, Rebekah, Rachel, Miriam, Deborah, Tamar, and Esther.

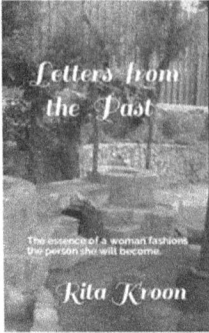

ISBN: 9780989198578

Discover God through His Attributes A to Z is an inspirational book meant to guide you in the search for a deeper and more meaningful relationship with God. Discover who He is. Be filled with wonder. Give praise to the Creator of the heavens and the earth. Reverence Him and be in awe, for there is no other god or anything in the entire universe like Him. Worship the King of kings in the splendor of His holiness. Rejoice that the Lord is one God as you discover the Father, Son, and Holy Spirit through His attributes.

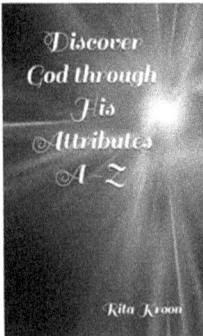

ISBN: 9780989198523

116

John – A Mini Study is a thirteen-week, interactive Bible study of the Gospel of John. It is suitable for individual or group setting in an Observation-Interpretation-Application method of study in an easy-to-read format. One way to think of it is like this: The observation of facts is like reading a menu; the interpretation is looking at the number of calories or the price on the menu. Each application question is the main course – the most satisfying part of the meal that energizes us for action. Each lesson has a principle that helps to keep the participants focused on what the author is trying to convey.

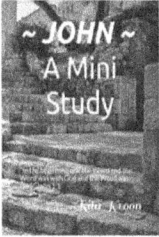

We learn what we can, apply what we know, and leave the rest to God.

"This is the disciple who testifies of these things and wrote these things, and we know this testimony is true." John 21:24 "BEHOLD! The Lamb of God!"

ISBN: 9798545633234

Nuggets From My Pocket is a collection of tidbits of wisdom quotes, sayings, blessings, promises and more that have been gathered along the trail. These gems of truth will inspire and encourage you. They will give you cause to pause, time to wonder and ponder, and a reason to reflect.

Nuggets From My Pocket is my gift to you for your pocket, or to share a nugget of encouragement with those around you

Here's a nugget to ponder: "God gives evidence of His existence, but not proof since He always leaves room for faith." **ISBN: 9780989198592**

More Nuggets From My Pocket is a collection of sayings, wit, insights, quotes, wisdom, promises, prayer, and more that were gathered where the trail led to an open meadow.

These gems will inspire you and encourage you no matter what path of life you travel. Stop to ponder the insights given, or to discover a fresh perspective, or to glean new meaning to old sayings.

More Nuggets From My Pocket is my way of giving you such an opportunity to explore rather than to merely hurry on your way. You may even want to share a nugget with a friend to encourage along the way.

ISBN: 9798682187225

Extra Nuggets From My Pocket is a collection of sayings meant to stir your imagination, fill your heart, and satisfy your desire for fresh "Ah, moments."

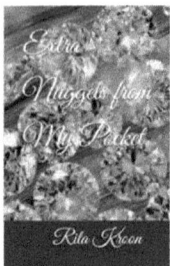

When the path of life leads me beside still waters, I search the beach for Extra Nuggets like one does when looking for agates on the North Shore. Some of these gems of truth, wit, quotes, prayers, blessings, and more are mine and some are those I gathered along the way and tucked into my pocket.

Come, walk with me along the beach and discover your *Extra Nuggets From My Pocket* for your pocket or to share with a friend. **ISBN: 9798587330566**

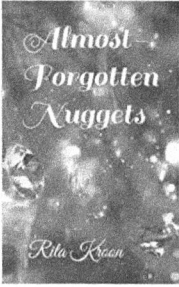

Almost-Forgotten Nuggets is a collection of truthful, inspiring, and wise sayings, and follows the footprints of its three siblings, ***Nuggets From My Pocket, More Nuggets From My Pocket,*** **and** ***Extra Nuggets From My Pocket.*** The path is familiar, but the landscape has an added dimension of newness that makes a pleasant journey most memorable. ***Almost-Forgotten Nuggets*** is sure to take you on an adventure much like a treasure hunt where one seeks the next gem to keep for your pocket or to share with a friend along the way.

Here is a preview of what is inside - "Unconfessed sin is like a math problem: it divides the heart; adds woes; subtracts peace, and it multiplies consequences."

Another peek – "It is sometimes difficult, but always good, to trust God with who you treasure most in this world."

ISBN: 9798511772042

Pebbles of Truth is a collection of short, timeless sayings of truth that are filled with wisdom, give great insight, plus unforgettable quotes, encouragement, blessings, thoughts to remember, and explore God's greatness. These pebbles of truth connect the heart with one's imagination much like pebbles on a beach connect the water and the land.

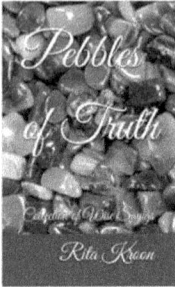

Here is a sneak peek: "Learn to write your hurts in the sand and to carve your blessings in stone." Here's another: "Man contributed nothing to his salvation except the sin that made it necessary."

Pebbles of Truth is sure to give you a delightful reading and sharing experience.

ISBN: 9798842917037

A Walk to the Well -
A place where women can find
Encouragement, Hope, and Inspiration
through the Blog and Books

www. awalktothewell.com